TALBOT J. TAYLOR

CHILDREN TALKING ABOUT TALKING
THE REFLEXIVE EMERGENCE OF LANGUAGE

Collected Papers Volume III

Edited by David Bade

International Association for the Integrational Study of
Language and Communication

Acknowledgements
"Rethinking Language Acquisition: What children learn" (with S.G. Shanker). Originally published in *Rethinking Linguistics* (H. Davis and T.J. Taylor, eds.). London: Routledge, ©2003.
"Where does language come from? The role of reflexive enculturation in language development". Originally published in *Language Sciences*, 32/1, pp. 14-27, ©2010.
"Language development and the integrationist". Originally published in *Language Sciences*, 33/4, pp. 579-583, ©2011.
 "Understanding others and understanding language: How do children do it?". Originally published in *Language Sciences*, 34/1, pp. 1-12, ©2012.
"Calibrating the child for language: Meredith Williams on a Wittgensteinian approach to language socialization". Originally published in *Language Sciences*, vol. 40, pp. 308-320, ©2013.
"Metalinguistic exchanges in child language development." (with Jasper C. van den Herik) Originally published in *Language Sciences*, v.88, ©2021.
Cover art: Self-portrait by Margaret Taylor (age 4).

Contents

I

Rethinking Language Acquisition:
What Children Learn
(with S.G. Shanker)

One way of thinking about the study of language acquisition is to see it as concerned with questions that are divisible into two major kinds. On the one hand, there are questions concerning what the child acquires. And then, there are questions about how the child acquires it. We will refer to these two types of question about language development as the WHAT question and the HOW question. Given this way of dividing the territory, any rethinking of the topic of language acquisition should begin with the WHAT question, because it lays the groundwork for the HOW question and, so, for the ways that we might approach the latter. At the same time, we should resist the commonsense view that the WHAT question is really very simple and that it is the HOW question that poses all the difficulties.

Q: "What does the child learn?"
A: "Why, the language of her community, of course."

Q: "How does she learn this language?"
A: "Well, different theorists have different ideas about that....."

However, on reflection, we can see that there is in fact a wide variety of ways that the WHAT question might be answered. What does the child learn? Well, she learns English, or Swahili, or Pitjantjatjara, or Mohawk, etc. Or, another answer might be: She learns the phonology, morphology, syntax, and lexicon of the English language. (For the purposes of this general, meta-methodological discussion, we will make all our references to the acquisition of English, although with the presupposition that the major points in the discussion could be addressed to the acquisition of any language.) Or, she acquires the ability to speak and understand English. Or, she learns how to make statements and commands, to ask questions, to make requests, to express her desires, etc., in English. Or, she learns what English words and grammatical constructions mean and how to use them with those meanings. Or, she learns the recursive processes of English sentence formation which enable her to produce and understand new sentences. Or, she learns to distinguish grammatical from ungrammatical combinations of English words. Or, she learns which positions to set the parameters of Universal Grammar to conform with the computational system of English. And so on.

It is worth emphasizing an important methodological implication: each such answer to the WHAT question determines the kind of HOW question that acquisition researchers will see themselves as concerned with. In other words, it will determine the kinds of explanations of language development that will be looked for and the criteria by which those explanations will be evaluated. If we answer the WHAT question (1w) 'She learns the grammar and lexicon of English', the HOW question (1h) that will then concern us is 'HOW does she learn the grammar and lexicon of English?'. If we answer the WHAT question (2w) 'She learns how to make statements and commands, ask questions, make requests, express her thoughts, etc.', then the HOW question (2h) which will occupy us will be 'HOW does she learn to do these things?'. Furthermore, each such HOW question raises different corollaries. The HOW question (1h) leads us to ask how the child can get information about the grammar and lexicon of English, whether that information is sufficient, how the child processes the information, what the obstacles are to this task, etc. Whereas the HOW question (2h) suggests different corollaries, concerning the means available and obstacles presented to the child who is learning to perform these speech acts. Moreover, it is clear that the kind of reply that might be seen as a satisfactory answer – or partial answer – to (1h) is of a very different sort than might be seen as a satisfactory answer to (2h), and this applies to any HOW question whose import might be motivated by a given conception of WHAT the child acquires. In sum, the way in which acquisition researchers answer the WHAT question determines what they will see as their investigational task, as well as the kind of research methods, hypotheses, evidence, and assumptions that they see as relevant to that task.

* * * *

The importance of this general point is easily illustrated by the approach to language development taken within generative linguistics. From the generativist perspective, WHAT a child eventually acquires (the adult competence referred to as 'the steady state, S_s') is a complex, formal system of core and peripheral knowledge—knowledge that has an anatomical realization in brain structure. It is understandable, therefore, that the basic principle of the generativist view of language

9

acquisition is that the study of HOW a child acquires language belongs, not to psychology, but rather, to biology, cognitive neuroscience, and Artificial Intelligence—with linguistics seen as a subfield of biology. For language acquisition is seen as "a matter of growth and maturation of relatively fixed capacities, ... largely determined by internal factors" (Chomsky 1966: 65). That is, a child need only be exposed to the 'right' kind of environment in order to allow for the information stored in the 'language gene(s)' to be activated. Hence, from the generativist perspective, the HOW question relates to the development of those internal, neurological structures in which that information is encoded and the mechanisms whereby it is processed. 'In certain fundamental respects we do not really learn language; rather, grammar grows in the mind' (Chomsky, 1980, p. 64).

In this light, we should note the connection between this conception of HOW children acquire language and Chomsky's formulation of the 'poverty of the stimulus' argument. This argument claims that, given the formally complex and internalized version of WHAT the child acquires (S_s), the child's experience does not—cannot—provide the kind of information, nor enough of it, to make it possible for the child to acquire it. And yet, *ex hypothesi*, she *does* acquire it. Indeed, generativism is committed to the principle that, strictly speaking, a child cannot *learn* language. For according to the poverty of the stimulus argument, a young child's knowledge that, e.g., anaphors are bound within a clause, could not be learned inductively. Similarly, if this internalized knowledge of the 'abstract principles of language' (as defined by generativism) is not neurologically present at birth—as is said to be the case in the child suffering from Specific Language Impairment (SLI)—then that knowledge *cannot* be acquired by training or practice (Gopnik et al. 1997).[1] The poverty of the stimulus argument therefore stands as the keystone in the generativist conception of HOW the child acquires internalized grammatical knowledge: since experiential learning is inadequate in helping the normal child move from her initial state, S_0, to the steady state, S_s, the child must therefore rely on 'internal factors'—certain kinds of innate knowledge—which determine the growth and maturation from S_0 to S_s .

In earlier stages of generativist thinking, the neurologically-realized grammar which the child eventually develops was thought to consist in a lexicon and in different kinds of rules determining the possible combinations of the lexical items. Given this early conception of WHAT the child acquires, the generativist interested in language acquisition attempted to determine HOW children acquire it: that is, HOW they acquire an internalized grammar thus defined in terms of knowledge of rules and a lexicon. Since the poverty of the stimulus argument concludes that grammatical knowledge cannot be learned merely by inductive methods, therefore the attempt to answer the HOW question was refocused as an inquiry into the properties that an innate language faculty requires so that it can derive the rules of the language from the limited information provided by experience. However, over the next few decades, generativist thinking went through changes concerning the structural properties of the competent

---

[1] For example, a normal child is said to construct an implicit rule for extracting regular inflectional endings from the language that she hears, whereas a child with SLI is unable to construct such implicit rules for morphological processes: all inflectional forms are learned on a case-by-case basis. Thus, whereas the normal child is said to acquire these abstract rules without any formal instruction and to apply them unconsciously, automatically, and effortlessly, the SLI child must memorize regular as well as irregular inflectional endings (i.e., store inflected forms as unanalyzed wholes for regular as well as irregular forms).

speaker/hearer's linguistic knowledge—i.e., concerning the content of S_s. Grammar came to be seen not so much as a matter of recursive rules whose job is to generate all-and-only the grammatical combinations of words in a language but rather of over-arching constraints whose task is to prevent any ungrammatical combinations. Along with these changes in the specification of WHAT the child acquires, so also did generativist claims concerning HOW the child acquired them: specifically, claims concerning the character of the innate, grammar-forming principles that are assumed to be part of the child's initial state S_0. In other words, as generativist thinking about WHAT the child acquires changed, so, necessarily, did generativist hypotheses concerning HOW this occurs.

While different conceptions of WHAT the child acquires lead ineluctably to contrasting accounts of HOW it is acquired, the reverse is not always true. For instance, generativist, social interactionist, and cognitivist explanations of language acquisition are quite different. However, the salient differences in their accounts of HOW the child acquires language are not matched by fundamental differences concerning their conceptions of WHAT is acquired.

Social interactionist models of language acquisition reject the 'poverty of the stimulus' argument and maintain that, on the contrary, the child's experience *does* provide more information to the acquisition process than that argument assumes (see Gallaway & Richards 1994). Thus social interactionists such as Jerome Bruner, Charles Ferguson, and Catherine Snow set out to show that speech directed to a child (CDS or 'motherese') is much different from adult speech and much different from the way that Chomsky had described it in the 'poverty of the stimulus' argument. In particular, they showed that CDS is syntactically and semantically simpler, grammatically more 'correct', and more fluent than Chomsky claimed. They also showed that there is a significant correlation between a caregiver's utterances and the child's preceding behaviour (e.g. vocalizations, gestures, gaze), as well as between the child's subsequent behaviour and the preceding caregiver utterance. These and other features of CDS were claimed to provide children with an environmental resource of information that 'scaffolds' their acquisition of linguistic knowledge, including the acquisition of many features of linguistic knowledge which generativist theorists had claimed to be impossible to acquire without an innate language acquisition device.

For instance, one of the most powerful predictors of a child's later linguistic ability is the proportion of maternal utterances that are semantically related to the preceding child utterances. In the past decade, researchers have started to discover more specific correlations: e.g. between a child's auxiliary verb use and the frequency of yes-no questions in which an auxiliary is preposed; the growth of a child's auxiliary verb use and the frequency with which caregivers expand child's utterances; the amount of maternal talk and the child's vocabulary growth; and the child's mastery of particular structures (e.g. passives, relative clauses) and the frequency with which these are used by the caregiver (see Gallaway & Richards 1994; Owens 1996).

Also standing in opposition to the generativist approach to language development is that of cognitivist linguistics. Cognitive linguistics is a broad church, but the following two examples should be sufficient to illustrate the point we are trying to make. An early cognitivist theory of acquisition was articulated by Roger Brown (Brown 1973), who discovered that, for English-speakers, grammatical morphology is acquired in a fairly regular order. But why, e.g., does a child acquire the progressive *ing* before she acquires the possessive *'s*? Rather than making the easy assumption that order of acquisition is simply determined by an innate language faculty,

Brown looked at two possible explanations: the frequency hypothesis and the cognitive complexity hypothesis. According to the former, acquisition is determined by the frequency of the morpheme in the caregiver's speech. But close study of parents' speech patterns did not bear this out. So attention shifted to the cognitive complexity hypothesis. Brown argued that the order of morphological development could be accounted for in terms of the cognitive complexity of the concept or structure involved. For instance, the concept of *in* is said to be easier for the child to grasp than that of *behind*. Accordingly, Brown hypothesized that it is because of its greater cognitive complexity that *behind* is typically acquired after *in*.

Not surprisingly, critics quickly drew attention to the fact that Brown's cognitivist argument has a distinctly circular feeling. How is one to determine a criterion for 'cognitive complexity' that is independent of acquisition order? Or does a construction's cognitive complexity simply boil down to the fact that it appears later in development? How else can one measure cognitive complexity? Worse: the cognitive complexity criterion does not mesh well with cross-linguistic findings. For certain constructions that appear relatively late for English-speakers—e.g. passives—appear quite early for other language-speakers (Crago et al. 1997). At the same time, the cognitivist premise is challenged by generativist arguments about linguistic savants (cognitively impaired children with age-matched language abilities) and about children with selective impairments (cognitively age-matched children with significant language deficits). These populations are said to demonstrate that acquisition of language proceeds independently of cognition and that it is therefore an autonomous, maturational phenomenon (Pinker 1994).

In any case, whether one accepts the cognitivist or generativist account of HOW morphemes are learned, the relevant point here is that both accounts share a common view of

WHAT is learned: viz. meaning-bearing formal units (known variously as 'morphemes', 'formants', 'signs', or 'lexical entries' in the literature). These are viewed as discrete, self-contained, code-defined units, each possessing a distinct form and meaning and having an existence independent of any particular act of speech. With regard to the acquisition of morphemes, the cognitivist Brown and the generativists do not disagree over WHAT is acquired, but only HOW it is acquired.

A more recent example of a cognitivist theory is that proposed by Michael Tomasello (cf. Tomasello 1999). Tomasello takes the task of acquiring grammatical constructions to be guided by general cognitive predispositions, in particular, the child's ability to recognize—and so imitate—the relations and event schemas to which her caregivers attempt to draw her attention by their use of particular grammatical constructions.

> Fundamentally, the way the child learns a concrete linguistic construction ... is the same way she learns words: she must understand which aspects of the joint attentional scene the adult intends for her to attend to when using this linguistic construction, and then culturally (imitatively) learn that construction for that communicative function. (Tomasello 1999:143)

Imagine, for instance, that one of the aspects of the perceptual scene to which the adult intends the child to attend is the cognitive relationship of agent-patient, holding between two of the items in that scene: e.g., the dog is biting the postman. Furthermore, the adult signifies this communicative intention by using an SVO construction: i.e., he says "Hey, Fido is biting the postman". In this case, the child's ability to recognize the adult's communicative intention will facilitate her acquisition of the SVO construction. When she herself next has the communicative intention of drawing her hearer's attention to an agent-patient relation, she will imitatively use an SVO construction to do so. Accordingly, the way a child acquires such grammatical knowledge is not a matter of computational processes which mechanically deduce the rules for generating well-formed formulae. Rather, grammatical knowledge is acquired by means of role-reversal imitation, by means of which the child learns to use particular grammatical constructions to express her communicative intentions (see further discussion of this in Joseph, Love, and Taylor 2001, ch.12). What Tomasello calls "functionally based distributional analysis" is therefore founded on the general, cognitivist assumption that "the child must learn that the various linguistic symbols in a complex utterance partition the referential scene into isolable perceptual/conceptual elements, and that these two sets of elements—the symbolic and the referential—must be aligned appropriately". (Tomasello 1999:145)

> Human children are not innately equipped with a universal grammar applicable to all of the languages of the world equally. They are adapted to enter into joint attentional interactions with adults and to understand adult intentions and attention – and eventually to adopt adult roles in these interactions, including their use of particular linguistic conventions. (Tomasello 2001:36)

However, as with Brown's theory of acquisition order, one cannot ignore the whiff of circularity in Tomasello's cognitivist account of the acquisition of grammatical constructions. For how, independently of the properties of the utterance expressing it, is the acquisition researcher to identify the properties of a communicative intention? How is the researcher to determine what the cognitive relations, schemas, elements, and structures are to which competent speakers intend their hearers to attend and with which the symbols in their utterance are aligned — *except* by taking the relations, schemas, elements, and structures of their utterances as transparent reflections of that cognitive content?

All the same, from the point of view of this chapter's argument what is most important here is that, regardless of the differences between cognitivists, social interactionists, and generativists on HOW grammatical constructions are acquired—whether by means of cognitive, 'mindreading' predispositions, by 'motherese' and interactional 'scaffolding', or by means of an innate grammar-deducing faculty—these three theoretical schools share a common view of the nature of (the grammatical aspect of) WHAT is acquired. What the child acquires is knowledge of the grammatical constructions of her language: e.g., SVO structures, auxiliary + verb structures, passive structures, morphological structures (such as noun inflection), head + modifier structures, etc. Although we would not want to ignore the important differences between the cognitivist and the generativist models of grammar—in particular, the cognitivist does not take grammatical constructions to be well-formed formulae but symbolic devices for expressing communicative intentions—nevertheless, they share, along with the social interactionist, the general assumption that WHAT a child acquires in acquiring a language is *a grammar*, conceived as *internally-realized knowledge* of a complex system of units (morphemes, words, signs, lexical entries, etc.) and the combinatorial relations between them.

The claim being made here, on the other hand, is that for the advances to be made in the study and explanation of language acquisition, there must now be some 'rethinking' about WHAT it is that the child acquires in acquiring language. Different approaches to the HOW question will fail to make appreciable advances unless and until this is done. Because the WHAT question is methodologically prior to the

HOW question, new breakthroughs in explaining how children develop language wait upon a different way of conceptualizing what it is that the child acquires in becoming linguistically and communicationally competent.

* * * *

There is another, related set of ways in which the WHAT question influences attempts to explain HOW language is acquired. Often, assumptions about what the child *eventually* acquires are read 'retroactively' into claims about what the child is acquiring at an *earlier* stage in her development, whether this is at 3 months old or 6 months or 18 months or 3 years. For example, given a child who at an early age begins doing a recognizable form of behaviour—say, at 9 months she extends her arm and/or finger in the direction of toy—this is often taken as showing that she now is *already* performing a gestural version of a linguistic act which every human, all things being equal, eventually learns to do: namely (in this example), she is referring to the toy. As seductive as this way of describing early child behaviour is, the study and explanation of HOW children learn is vitiated if it is taken for granted that WHAT they will eventually learn—to refer, to mean such-and-such by a given word, to follow particular rules, to request, to say what they are thinking, etc.—is already present in germinal forms in their early communicative behaviour, only needing conventional refinement and normalization as the child matures.

Let us consider in more depth an illustrative example of the effects of taking a retroactive perspective. All normal children growing up in an English-speaking culture learn how to make what are called 'requests': that is, they learn how to 'ask for' things that they want and for actions that they want others to perform for them. Moreover, they typically learn a variety of ways of asking for things and actions. In other

18

words, the speech act of requesting (or asking-for) is one feature of WHAT the child is thought eventually to acquire in becoming a fully competent speaker/hearer of English.

Now, as many acquisition researchers have noted, most children in the second half of their first year develop a gestural complex which involves extending a hand (or both hands) in the direction of some (presumably desired) object while directing their gaze to the eyes of the person who might be able to obtain the object for them—often accompanying this gesture with 'fretting' noises or even what is called a 'phonetically consistent form'. In many studies of the acquisition of requests (e.g., Bruner, Roy, and Ratner 1982, Masur 1983, Zinober and Martlew 1985, Griffiths 1985, Ervin-Tripp and Gordon 1986, Wootton 1997), this gestural complex (open hand extended, fretting, mutual gaze) is treated as an early instance of a request, that is, of that speech act which is a universal feature of every adult English speaker's competence. The general view propounded in these studies is that the behavioural components of the child's early request will, over time, be reshaped, verbalized, and socially normalized until it more nearly approximates the conventional form of an adult English speaker's request. Accordingly, in such studies, the 9 month-old is described as "requesting" and as "asking for" things—in other words, she is described as if she were producing instances of the same communicational act which 5 year-olds and adults produce, but in an early, 'primitive', only-partly-conventionalized form. Such studies therefore 'retroactively' interpret the child's behavior at 9 months as *already* a request, although not yet one which has all the properties that an adult speaker's request would have. A request, nonetheless, is WHAT the 9 month-old has produced.

Countless, similar claims can be found in the language acquisition literature concerning the child's early instances of acts of reference, of meaning, of following particular rules, of offering, of grasping the meanings of particular words, etc. For instance, a child's early utterance of [dɔgi] will be described as "referring" to a particular dog in the contextual environs. Her utterance of [bɪg dɔgi] will be characterized as an early instance of the modifier + head construction (or of following the rule that modifiers come before heads). Or when she utters [dædi] upon hearing the front door close, she will be described as meaning that her father has come home. Doubtless, these acts are all within the competence of the older child. In other words, all things being equal the child in question *will* learn how to refer to things, to request, to combine modifiers and with the words they modify, and to say what she means. This in turn fuels our inclination to characterize the younger child's behaviour using the same metalinguistic expressions. However, there are potential dangers in this 'retroactive' way of studying child language development and, even more important, a possibility of serious conceptual and methodological confusions.

In the first place, we should note one unfortunate and misleading effect that describing the 9 month-old's behaviour as 'a request' can have on child language research. It can steer investigative programmes away from looking at the child's behaviour in its own, context-specific terms – that is, away from looking at the ways in which, at a given age, the child's behaviour can be observed to function in the interactions in which it is produced. In other words, if the acquisition researcher studying the videotapes of a nine-month-old takes the child to have produced an instance of one of the speech act types in the adult's repertoire—albeit an immature token of this speech act—then he has a readymade answer to the WHAT question. "What was that behaviour (REACH + FRET + MUTUAL GAZE) she just produced? Ah, a request, of course". Given this seductive power of this methodological shortcut, the motivation to inquire any further into the WHAT question is sharply reduced. Would it not seem pointless and redundant for the researcher to persist in asking how a child's behaviour functions in a given interaction, WHAT it is *for her* in that interaction, if the answer—a request—is apparently already available? This is just what commits us to a particular way of looking at the matter. The WHAT question seems already to have its answer; so the researcher is compelled to move on to the next question: HOW does the child acquire this ability? How, so early in her life, does a prelinguistic, nine-month-old child learn to request?

> *The decisive movement in the conjuring trick has been made, and it was the very one that we thought quite innocent.* (Wittgenstein 1953 §308)

In contrast to this *retroactive* perspective, Alan Fogel's research is an example of a research programme that approaches communicational development from a more *progressive* perspective. Fogel takes communication to be a 'co-regulative' process, a term which is intended to highlight the nonlinear nature of continuous mutual adjustment. The actions of communicating partners are fundamentally relational, as partners mutually adjust their behaviors to each other in subtle ways. Thus, communication, according to Fogel, cannot be reduced to a single modality, or to the summation of multiple modalities.

In his *Developing through Relationships*, Fogel provides a micro-analysis of the first time Andrew, a one-year old infant, voluntarily releases an object into his mother's hand.

> First, his arm extends...and then he releases the object. In past weeks, Andrew has extended his arm many times toward his mother without releasing the object. (But, on this occasion) once Andrew's arm is extended

his hand remains relatively stationary and gradually opens as mother's hand moves underneath his hand. The fork gently leaves Andrew's hand as it is pulled only by the slightest contact with the mother's moving palm. The object release, therefore, is not entirely due to Andrew's initiative. Since the child does not actually drop the object into the mother's hand and the mother does not actually take hold of the object, the object transfer seems to be jointly constructed by both, a genuinely co-regulated activity (Fogel 1993: 21).

It would be misleading to describe the child's action in Fogel's example as an early instance of Andrew 'giving' or 'offering' an object to another, just as it is misleading to study a child's early REACH + FRET + MUTUAL GAZE as 'an early version of a request'. But Fogel's frame-by-frame analyses look at how the child's behaviour functions in his interactions at one year. They characterize WHAT the child is doing at that time in terms of the interactions in which he produces it, rather than as an early instance of a type of act that he will later be able to produce adult versions of. Fogel's description in the passage above reveals how Andrew's actions are subtly integrated, moment by moment, with those of his mother, which are, in turn, designed in response to his actions. What emerges from Fogel's patient analysis is that the passing of the fork from son to mother is as much the mother's action as it is the son's—a mutual accomplishment. The result is therefore better understood as a jointly managed, dynamically unfolding interaction, rather than as a sequence of discrete acts produced by two independent agents. From Fogel's perspective, WHAT each person does at any given moment appears as a non-discrete, co-produced component of a jointly managed endeavour. No behavioural segment is independent of the interaction as a jointly managed whole. It is the child's methods of integrating his behaviour into that jointly managed whole that develop over time, as do the integrational methods used by the mother. It is by tracing the increased sophistication of the methods by which child and caregiver integrate their behaviour that Fogel's progressive approach addresses the HOW questions of child development. What emerges is a picture of the child progressing by means of context-dependent, practical, purposive steps, each taken one at a time, rather than by advancing automatically (miraculously) down a species-defined path to a predetermined goal.

It cannot be denied, however, that such a progressive approach to development leaves a troubling question unanswered. How can interactional development, so understood, ever lead to the point at which we know all normal children eventually to arrive – that is, to the point where they produce true requests, offers, acts of reference and meaning, etc? At what point—if ever—does a child's means of integrating his behaviour into such jointly produced interactions somehow transform into the production of, e.g., discrete instances of true requests? All English-speaking children eventually produce requests; yet, if the REACH + FRET + MUTUAL GAZE gesture is not an early, germinal version of a request, then what must be added or changed so that the child will start producing true requests? To address this question, we need to look at a second reason why it is so misleading to take a retroactive perspective on language acquisition.

* * * *

WHAT is a request? Does it consist merely in the production of a particular behavioural complex? If not, then what more is there to requesting or asking for something than merely producing the sounds [pliz me ai hæv ə krækr]—which, of course, many parrots and computers can do? In addressing this question, we should reflect on the important fact that the adult who produces a request—who asks for something—not only can produce the behavioural components of a request, she can also contribute to and respond sensibly to another's reflexive discourse about her behaviour. That is, she is able to participate in reflexive interactions ('metadiscourse') about her communicational acts. Such a reflexive interaction is predicated on the mutual acknowledgement of WHAT she is doing— namely, in the present example, that which in English-speaking cultures we call "requesting" or "asking for" something— and of its implications. For example, the adult speaker of English is able to make sense of or make an adequate reply to such questions as "Is *this* what you're asking for?", "Are you *asking* me for that or just showing it to me?", "Why do you want this?", "What do you mean?", and a host of other metadiscursive remarks that treat what she has just done *as an intended instance of a request*. She knows how to explain the act that she has just produced and how to confirm or object to the understanding of her act that is manifested in her addressee's response: e.g., A: "Don't tell me what to do!"; B: "I wasn't telling you; I was merely asking." Her ability to produce a request is inseparable from her ability to participate in the metadiscursive 'support-mechanism' provided by such reflexive practices and without which the act of requesting could have no cultural existence. (How could there be the act of requesting in a culture in which no such metadiscursive practices existed? That is, in a form of life in which one could never speak of a behavioural product as a request, or of its interactional implications, or of its understanding or misunderstanding, etc.? See Taylor 2000.)

So there is this important difference between a 9 month-old's REACH + FRET + MUTUAL GAZE gesture and an adult's request. If you ask "Is this what you are asking for?", an adult—but not a child—can reply "No, it's the other one" or "Yes, that's the one". Or if you ask "Are you asking me to get that for you?", the adult—but not the child—can reply "Yes, would you please" or "No, I'm showing you the object I just mentioned". And so on. A competent speaker of English is able not only to do what the young child can do—namely, produce the behavioural components of a request—the competent speaker of English is also able to participate effectively in reflexive discourse which is predicated on *the recognition of her behaviour as an intended instance of a request.*

In reflexive discourse cultural members articulate their conception of what they are doing, have done, will do, tried to do, might do, etc. By 'articulate their conception', we simply mean here that, from time to time, they speak of their own or others' behaviour as instances of culturally-recognized communicational acts. And they reply sensibly to another's characterization of their own or someone else's behaviour in such terms, e.g., as a request, as 'asking for' something, as being about something, as meaning something, as offering, as being the same as what someone else just said, as making sense or not making sense, and so on. If a speaker produced behaviour that had the superficial components of, e.g., a request and yet she could not participate competently in reflexive discourse— could not, for instance, articulate her conception of what she was trying to do as 'asking for' something—there would be salient grounds for doubting whether, as we say colloquially, she 'knew what she was doing' in behaving as she was. To put it another way: if this person's behaviour, because she cannot yet participate in reflexive discourse, shows no indication that she herself conceives of what she is doing *as a request*, then on what grounds can we legitimately insist that, nevertheless, she has produced an instance of a request? What sense is there in attributing the production of a particular cultural-communicational act to someone who has no conception of the act in question?[2]

The general point being made here is that to request (to ask-for) is a reflexive, culturally constructed, communicational act-category. The act of requesting (asking-for) may therefore be thought of as a hybrid of behavioural activity and cultural construction. The members of English-speaking cultures continually construct and maintain this act-category *metadiscursively*, that is, by speaking, writing, and signing about particular forms of behaviour *as* instances of 'requesting' or 'asking for' something and by responding in certain culturally familiar ways to such characterizations. A request is not a request *sui generis*: that is, a certain gestural, or vocal, or written complex is not in-and-of-itself a request, simply by virtue of its behavioural properties. For such a behavioural complex to be an instance of a request, the act-category of 'request' must already be culturally recognized: that is, acts of requesting and the implications of producing requests must be recognizable topics of the culture's reflexive practices and meta-discourse.

The reflexive character of requesting leads, in turn, to the conclusion that the ability to produce an instance of a request requires at least some competence in that culture's reflexive practices. *The competent speaker's ability to produce an instance of the speech act of request is therefore inseparable from her ability to participate in such reflexive practices.* Furthermore, this general point holds for any languacultural act: referring, meaning something by a word or sentence, using

---

[2] This is the same kind of question that is addressed to claims about the understanding of a chimpanzee who can sign 'apple' when you show him an apple, but cannot respond competently to a signed request for an apple or to the questions "Where is the apple?" or "Is this an apple I'm holding?" See Savage-Rumbaugh, Shanker, and Taylor, 1998

a particular grammatical construction, understanding a sign as meaning such-and-such, saying the same thing as someone else said, and so on. Once we recognize the cultural construction of these foundational 'things we do with words', then it should become clear that learning to do any one of them involves more than just mastering the production of a certain behavioural complex. It also necessarily involves initiation into the reflexive cultural practices in which they have their roots.

It should by now be clear that for a child to learn how to request—to refer, to mean such-and-such by a given word, to use a particular grammatical construction, etc.—it is not enough that she learn to produce conventionalized patterns of behaviour. She must also learn how to participate in reflexive discourse predicated on the recognition of these as particular kinds of communicational acts. The development of her ability to produce instances of these communicational acts depends upon the development of her ability to participate in reflexive practices concerning those acts.

Language has an inherently reflexive character, the implication of which is that language is more than just a natural form of human behaviour—it is a cultural practice. Language acquisition involves *both* increasingly sophisticated and normalized forms of behaviour *and* initiation into the reflexive practices by which the speaker's culture determines WHAT particular behavioural complexes *count as instances of*, including what they mean. Therefore, to learn HOW to request (or to refer to something, or to mean such-and-such, or to use a particular grammatical construction), a child must do more than refine her behavioural skills, she must undergo this cultural initiation.

* * * *

The clear implication of this argument is that we need to rethink WHAT it is that children acquire in acquiring language

27

and, the particular point argued in this paper, we need to resist the temptation to take a 'retroactive' perspective on the child's communicational development. The retroactive perspective is misleading for at least the two reasons discussed here. It invites the researcher to ignore the interactional character of a child's behaviour at the time and in the circumstances of its production and also to treat as instances of mature linguistic acts early forms of action that may share the behavioural—but not the cultural-reflexive—characteristics of those acts.

This suggests, of course, that acquisition research should pay a great deal more attention than it has to the child's development of metadiscursive skills—that is, to the child's development of the ability to participate (either productively or comprehendingly) in reflexive interactions concerning the kinds of things that people do in communicational interaction. Moreover, the study of the child's acquisition of this ability should look not for the automatic unfolding of some kind of species-determined programme of reflexive awareness. Rather, it should focus on particular instances of the child's integration of metadiscursive techniques into her forms of participation in and contribution to jointly-managed interactions. Some illustrative examples of this approach may be seen in the studies of the child's developing use of sequential knowledge and 'understandings' that are presented in Tony Wootton's *Interaction and the Development of Mind* (1997).

Reflexive abilities are sometimes referred to as 'second order', because they concern *talking about* the products of talking itself. And yet, the point being made here is that the development of these 'second order' abilities is an *inseparable* part of the child's development of her 'first order' abilities, those which have always been the main focus of research on language acquisition: that is, with the child's abilities to request, to describe, to mean, to refer, to use particular grammatical constructions, etc. On reflection, one can see why this is so. For these 'first order' abilities concern the production of particular kinds of linguistic acts the characteristics of which are reflexively constructed and maintained by means of the culture's everyday discourse about what one does and can do in verbal interaction. It follows, then, that developing the ability to produce these acts involves not only learning the behavioural mechanics of producing them but also WHAT they are. Learning how to request, to refer, or to mean such-and-such is as much a matter of learning how to behave in certain ways as it is a matter of becoming a competent participant in meta-discourse concerning what someone 'asked for', what they were 'talking about', or what they 'meant'. These 'first order' and 'second order' aspects of language development are inseparable because it is only by means of their integration that there is a 'WHAT the child learns'.

References

Brown, R. (1973) *A First Language: The Early Stages.* Cambridge, MA: Harvard University Press.

Bruner, J.S., Roy, C. and Ratner, N. (1982) The beginnings of request. In K. Nelson (ed.) *Children's Language,* vol. III. New York: Gardner Press, pp. 91-138.

Chomsky, N. (1966) *Cartesian Linguistics: a Chapter in the History of Rationalist Thought.* New York: Harper and Row.

Chomsky, N. (1980) *Rules and Representations.* Oxford: Blackwell.

Crago, M.B., Shanley, E.M., Hough-Eyamie, A., and Hough-Eyamie, W. P. (1997) Exploring innateness through cultural and linguistic variation. In M. Gopnik (ed.), *The Inheritance and Innateness of Grammars* (pp. 70-90). New York: Oxford University Press.

Ervin-Tripp, S. and Gordon, D. (1986) The development of
requests. In R.L. Schiefelbusch (ed.) *Language Competence*. San Diego: College Hill Press. pp. 61-95.

Fogel, A. (1993) *Developing Through Relationships.*
Chicago: The University of Chicago Press.

Gallaway, C. and Richards, B.J. (1994) *Input and Interaction
in Language Acquisition.* Cambridge, Cambridge
University Press.

Gopnik, A., and Meltzoff, A. (1997) *Words, Thoughts, and
Theories.* Cambridge, MA: MIT Press.

Griffiths, P. (1985) The communicative functions of
children's single-word speech. In M. Barrett (ed.)
Children's Single Word Speech. Chichester: Wiley,
pp. 87-112.

Joseph, J., Love, N. and Taylor, T. (2001) *Landmarks in
Linguistic Thought II: The Western Tradition in the
Twentieth Century.* London: Routledge.

Masur, E.F. (1983) Gestural development, dual-directional
signalling and the transition to words. *Journal of Psycholinguistic Research*, 12:93-109.

Owens, R.E. (1996) *Language Development: An Introduction.* Boston: Allyn and Bacon.

Pinker, S. (1994) *The Language Instinct.* New York: William
Morrow and Company, Inc.

Savage-Rumbaugh, E.S., Shanker, S.G. and Taylor, T.J.
(1998) *Apes, Language and the Human Mind.* New
York: Oxford University Press.

Taylor, T.J. (2000) 'Language constructing language: the
implications of reflexivity for linguistic theory'.
Language Sciences 22, 483-99.

Tomasello, M. (1999) *The Cultural Origins of Human
Cognition.* Cambridge, MA: Harvard University
Press.

Tomasello, M. (2001) 'Bruner on Language Acquisition', in D. Bakhurst and S. Shanker (eds.), *Jerome Bruner: Language, Culture, Self*, 31-49. London: Sage.

Wittgenstein, L. (1953) *Philosophical Investigations*. Oxford: Basil Blackwell.

Wootton, A. J. (1997) *Interaction and the Development of Mind*. Cambridge: Cambridge University Press.

Zinober, B. and Martlew, M. (1985) The development of communicative gestures. In M. Barrett (ed.) *Children's Single-Word Speech*. London: Wiley, pp. 183-215.

II

Where does language come from? The role of reflexive enculturation in language development

Abstract

How does the developing child bridge the ontological gap from the empirical, measurable world of behavioral patterns, anatomical structures, and neurological processes to the world of the linguistic phenomena referred to by the expressions of commonsense metalinguistic discourse: words, meanings, names, truth, languages, understanding, and so on? Rejecting the positions both of sceptical eliminativism and of linguistic immanence, this paper argues that the linguistic identity of language emerges only gradually, by means of the child's increasingly competent participation in the discursive processes of reflexive enculturation.

Ontology thus recapitulates methodology. And anthropology loses its object. The properties of culture having been ignored in the practice of its explanation, it is presumed that these properties have no autonomy or value as such—which is a rationalization of the fact that the explanation cannot account for them. (Sahlins, 1977, p. 89)

1. Ontological schizophrenia in the study of child development

Western thought in the modern period can be characterized as suffering from a particular kind of rhetorical affliction, one which Marshall Sahlins has termed 'ontological schizophrenia' (Sahlins, 1977, p. 84). The source of this affliction is that human inquiry in the modern period has been driven by the logic of a dialogue opposing scepticism and commonsense. The study of language development is no exception.

From the perspective of (what is called) commonsense, children brought up, for example, in an Anglophone community learn such linguistic facts as

- that [pɪn] and [pɜn] are different words
- that [pɪn] and [piːn] are the same word
- that the word fortnight means 'two weeks'
- that *Milou* is the name of Tintin's dog
- that instead of ''The hamster me bit'', you should say ''The hamster bit me''
- that the expression *the pope* refers to a religious leader who lives in Rome
- that the neighbors speak a language called *Swahili*
- that the neighbors' aunt does not understand English

- that it's not true to say that your stomach hurts unless it really does

Children come to know these and very many other linguistic facts, and they acquire the skills for putting this knowledge to productive use.

However, in reply to such commonsense claims, the sceptic objects. Children, he says, obviously learn a great deal as they mature. *But they do not—indeed, could not possibly—learn these types of things*. No doubt, children do develop more and more complex forms of verbal behavior as they mature; and these behavioral developments necessarily entail equally complex developments of a physical and neurological kind, some of which we are able to observe and study empirically. All the same, insists the sceptic, it would be miraculous indeed if out of this empirical hat, children were somehow able to pull metaphysical rabbits. In other words, it is dangerously misleading to characterize behavioral, physical, and neurological maturation in terms of the development of things such as meanings, words, languages, rules, communicational intentions, acts of reference and understanding, and so on. For none of these things about which commonsense blithely assumes children to learn are—or even *could* be—empirical phenomena. Rather, they are mythological objects: cultural phantasms that are generated by naïve linguists taking folk metadiscourse too seriously. True, children who are learning language come to use and understand the expressions common to the metalinguistic discourse (or "metadiscourse") of their community. In an Anglophone community, such expressions may include *de dicto* versions of those listed above, i.e., expressions such as

- "No dear. The word I said was *pin*, not *pen*"
- "*Fortnight* means 'two weeks'"
- "*Milou* is the name of Tintin's dog"

- "You should say 'The hamster bit me', not 'The hamster me bit'"
- "When he said 'the pope', he was talking about a religious leader who lives in Rome"
- "Our neighbors speak a language called Swahili"
- "Their aunt didn't understand what you said"
- "It's not true to say that your stomach hurts unless it really does"

Anglophone children come to understand very many such expressions of ordinary metadiscourse, and they acquire the skills for putting this knowledge to productive use. All the same, the sceptic asserts, it is scientifically irresponsible to take it for granted that the important place that folk metadiscourse has in our sociocultural lives entails that the expressions used in metadiscourse pick out real phenomena in the world: namely, meanings, words, languages, rules, intentions, acts of reference and understanding, and so on. For the developmental researcher to assume a priori that, in acquiring language, what it is that children acquire are these folk-cultural phantasms would be methodologically unsound, to say the least. Furthermore, the legacy of such unscientific assumptions is devastating for empirical research, for it puts the onus on those doing developmental research to explain how these metaphysical rabbits ever got into the hat in the first place. Alternatively, she must explain how the more mundane neurological and behavioral phenomena that can be empirically observed somehow mutate into the metaphysical entities and mythological events about which commonsense naively takes children to learn.

These dialogically opposed rhetorical strategies—commonsense and scepticism—have left the student of language acquisition facing an awkward question – a question that is at the heart of the ontological schizophrenia plaguing developmental research in the modern period:

> *How does the child get across the ontological gap from the empirical, measurable world of behavioral patterns, anatomical structures, and neurological processes to the linguistic world populated by the "emic" phenomena of metadiscursive commonsense?*

2. Sceptical acid heads

Good examples of the use and power of sceptical rhetoric can be found in the theoretical arguments advanced by cognitive eliminativists – in particular, those psychologists who adopt some version of behaviorism or cognitive physicalism. Thus, the behaviorist Watson (1913, 1924) argued that the notions that populate folk psychological discourse—such as 'belief', 'wish', 'know', 'desire', 'refer', 'understand'—are what he called "the heritages of a timid savage past", handed down, generation after generation, at mother's knee (Watson, 1924, p. 3). Such notions, Watson argued, ought to be assigned the same fate as was meted out, following the birth of modern chemistry, to alchemical notions such as 'phlogiston', 'caloric', and 'essences'. Instead, what psychologists studying human development should focus on is that which is (i) observable in behavior and (ii) identifiable in terms which do not rely on the projections of our folk myths.

In a similar vein, cognitive physicalists, like Paul and Patricia Churchland and Stephen Stich, argue that it is physical properties and processes in the brain which should be the ultimate explanatory objects for scientific psychology. Accordingly, folk psychological terms like "belief", "remember", "feel", "think", "desire", "prefer", "imagine", etc., should be eliminated from scientific discourse. Patricia Churchland warns that "folk psychology is false, and its ontology is chimerical" (Churchland, 1991, p. 65). Stephen Stich agrees: "Beliefs are myths", he says, "and it is no more sensible to inquire about [a man's] beliefs than to investigate whether he has an excess of phlegm or a deficiency of yellow bile" (Stich, 1983, p. 2). Another who argues against the reliance on folk terms in cognitive research is the philosopher Dan Dennett. He illustrates his argument with this colorful thought experiment:

> Suppose we find a society that lacks our knowledge of human physiology, and that speaks a language just like English except for one curious family of idioms. When they are tired, they talk of being beset by fatigues, of having mental fatigues, muscular fatigues, fatigues in the eyes and fatigues of the spirit. Their sports lore contains such maxims as "too many fatigues spoils your aim" and "five fatigues in the legs are worth ten in the arms". When we encounter them and tell them of our science, they want to know *what fatigues are*. They have been puzzling over such questions as whether numerically the same fatigue can come and go and return, whether fatigues have a definite location in matter and space and time, whether fatigues are identical with some particular physical states or processes or events in their bodies, or are made of some sort of stuff. We can see that they are off to a bad start with these questions, but what should we tell them? One thing we might tell them is *that there simply are no such things as fatigues* – they have a confused ontology. We can expect some of them to retort: "You don't think there are fatigues? Run around the block a few times and you'll know better! There are many things your science might teach us, but the non-existence of fatigues isn't one of them!" We ought to be unmoved by this retort. (. . .) Fatigues are not good theoretical entities,

however well entrenched the term "fatigues" is in the habits of thought of the imagined society. The same is true, I hold, of beliefs, desires, pains, mental images, experiences—as all these are ordinarily understood. Not only are beliefs and pains not good theoretical things (like electrons or neurons), but the *state-of-be-lieving-that-p* is not a well-defined or definable theoretical state. (Dennett, 1981, pp. xix–xx)

Now, from the perspective of the linguistic eliminativist, it is easy to see that, to Dennett's list of "bad theoretical entities"—such as 'beliefs', 'desires', and 'mental images'—one could add linguistic-theoretical entities such as 'meanings', 'words', 'languages', 'reference', 'truth', 'names', 'understanding', and so on. Naturally, the natives who inhabit the Anglophone linguistic community want to know "what these things are": that is, these "things" which are regularly mentioned in commonsense discourse about language in their community. However, in keeping with Dennett's recommendation for commonsense psychological things, we ought to be unmoved. For the natives in the Anglophone linguistic community have a confused ontology. Meanings, words, languages, names, and so on are not empirical phenomena. This linguistic ontology is at best a useful cultural fiction, but a fiction nonetheless. And linguistic science should not be the study of fictions, no matter how entrenched those fictions are in the habits of discourse among the ordinary members of the society. Nor, therefore, should the science of language development be the study of how children acquire such commonsense linguistic fictions: meanings, words, languages, understanding, etc. The conclusion of the linguistic eliminativist's argument is therefore rhetorically analogous to that of behaviorists like Watson and physicalists like the Churchlands and Stich: namely, scientists who study the child's linguistic development should focus their observations and explanations on the development of physical properties and processes in the brain and on their related behavioral consequences. In addition, they should refrain from characterizing the explanatory objects of their studies with folk metalinguistic expressions like "English", "meaning", "word", "true", "is about", "name", "implies", "understands", or any of the innumerable cultural variants that may be found in commonsense metadiscourse around the world.

In other words, to the awkward question posed above about how the child gets across the ontological gap from the physical and behavioral to the linguistic, the sceptical theorist has a stubborn yet simple reply:

> *"The answer is that she doesn't; and the sooner developmental research stops wasting its time and money trying to explain how she does, the sooner will real scientific progress begin".*

3. The dogma of linguistic immanence

While the rhetorical strategy of scepticism has fueled eliminativist theories, linguistic inquiry in the modern period has been no less influenced by the rhetoric of commonsense, deployed, in particular, as a powerful rebuttal to sceptically based arguments (real or imagined, see Taylor, 1992). For it has proved a highly effective move indeed to respond to linguistic scepticism with questions like the following:

- "Oh, Mr. Sceptic, so what you're saying doesn't actually mean anything then?"
- "So, does this mean you're not really talking about anything?"
- "OK, so I guess you don't understand anything I'm saying, do you?"

- "I see; in other words, you don't actually believe what you're saying is true, right?"
- "Hmmm. So even though we're having this fine conversation, neither of us speaks any languages, not even the English language?"

Even if a hardline eliminativist were able somehow to dodge these bruising accusations of hypocrisy, he can be squeezed into an even more awkward rhetorical position by putting the matter in more general terms: terms that make the *reductio* painfully clear:

- "OK, but consider if *everyone* went around, like you, insisting that they never understand anything that anyone says, that they themselves never talk *about* anything, and that nothing they say is true or false, or has any meaning, or consists in the words of a particular language? What if everyone said such things all the time and, moreover, *behaved in complete conformity with these claims*? What communicational goals could ever be achieved? Indeed, what would be left to hold together the cultural fabric of life? The impossibility of such an imaginary state-of-affairs reveals the ultimate absurdity of your sceptical attitude towards commonsense metadiscourse. I'm afraid, my unbelieving friend, that—on the contrary—the conclusion must be that at least some of these things you doubt are, in fact, *necessarily true*".

Given the compelling power of the rhetoric of common-sense, it is no wonder that sceptical strategies are used only sparingly in human inquiry, like a powerful acid applied in drops here and there; just enough to burn away the weaker parts of theoretical models, but not too much. For that would do more harm than good. Moreover, when sceptical strategies are applied more liberally—as in the arguments of behaviorists or cognitive physicalists—there is always a strong defense raised which draws on the commonsense certainties—"metalinguistic truisms"—which apparently are of a substance resistant to sceptical acid.

But where does this leave research on language development? For if we side with commonsense and take the sceptic to be wrong about the fictional character of metadiscursive commonsense, then we cannot escape facing some version of the general question raised above about the ''ontological gap'' in language development: namely, how does the developing child bridge the yawning gap from the empirical, measurable world of behavioral patterns, anatomical structures, and neurological processes to the world of the linguistic phenomena referred to by the expressions of commonsense metalinguistic discourse?

As a preface to their reply to this question, anti-sceptical theorists of language development begin by noting that children do not typically acquire any metalinguistic expressions until *after* they have already learned their names as well as many other words and meanings. Children do not have to be told what words are or that words have meanings or that you can talk about things that are not contextually present or that some things people say are true but false or that some people speak a different language from the one we speak, and so on. How, therefore, the anti-sceptical response continues, could children learn all this unless the "emic" identity of language were somehow already *immanent* in the empirical phenomena themselves: i.e., in the spoken, written, and signed utterances of the linguistic community? The philosopher John Searle adopts a version of (what I will call) "the dogma of linguistic immanence" in his book *The Construction of Social Reality* (1995). Language, he says, is "self-identifying". In the main body of his book, Searle argues that institutional realities such as money, property, marriage, legal systems, and so on, require language. Indeed, they "are constituted by" language. However, he claims that language itself is the exception to this. For, although also institutional, linguistic facts—such as the fact that *comely* is a word of the English language, that it means 'pleasant to look at' or that it is not the same word as *calmly*—these facts do not require language. Language does not require (meta)language in the same way that other institutional facts require language. Instead, as Searle puts it, language is

> precisely designed to be a self-identifying category of institutional facts. The child . . . learns to treat the sounds that come out of her own and others' mouths as. . . standing for, or meaning something, or representing something. (. . .) [L]anguage doesn't require language in order to be language because it already is language. (Searle, 1995, p. 73).

So, for example, it is because people regularly *speak* and *write* of them as such—and act in accord with these linguistic habits—that certain pieces of paper *are* dollar bills, euros, yen, or renminbi. Cultural patterns of discourse about these pieces of paper are constitutive of their identity as money. On the other hand, it is *not* because people speak or write of them as such that the sounds that come out of our mouths are particular words, have particular meanings, are items of this or that language, are grammatically correct or incorrect, refer to specific people or things, are true or are false, etc. On the contrary, the sounds that come out of our mouths just *are* those linguistic things, *sui generis*. And they apparently would still have that identity even if no one ever spoke or wrote of them as such. For their multifaceted linguistic identity is inherent in the vocal or graphic phenomena themselves, and it is the component facts of this immanent identity which children are presented with and come eventually to learn when acquiring their native language.

An offshoot of this dogma of linguistic immanence is the metalinguistic nativism advocated by those who take concepts such as 'meaning', 'understanding', 'word', 'reference', etc. to be innate – part of the human genetic endowment. Thus, Pinker (1994) represents children as coming into the world equipped with metalinguistic concepts, which they are predisposed to apply to the vocal behavior produced in their developmental environment. That is, the child born into any culture is already in some sense aware that the sounds its mother produces are instances of a particular language and that those sounds are therefore endowed with properties such as meaning, referentiality, truth, and grammar. Similarly, Macnamara (1982) claims that the child is innately predisposed to recognize the referential properties of language. Shwe and Markman (1999) assume that children have an innate concept of understanding what is meant by an utterance, while Wierzbicka includes the metalinguistic concepts 'word', 'true' and 'say' among the "innate and indefinable human concepts which provide the bedrock of human cognition and communication" (Wierzbicka, 2001, p. 507). (Of course, from the sceptic's perspective, such nativist affirmations are akin to saying that the metaphysical rabbit must have been an integral part of the millinery process by which the physical hat was originally made.)

The argument motivating this paper is that, in response to the question raised above about the ontological gap in explanations of linguistic development, both of these opposing theoretical schools are rhetorically evasive. That is, both immanence and eliminativist theories respond to the question by attempting simply to *wish it away*. On the one hand, the immanence theorist drapes himself in the rhetorical flag of commonsense and boldly asserts that the sceptical critique is wrong and that children *just do* get across that categorial gap. (Damn it – they must!) For after all, the immanence theorist insists, every child comes eventually to know a language, hundreds and hundreds of its words, the meanings of these words, and how combinations of words can be used to talk about things and events, assert truths, convey their intentions, etc. We should therefore take this feat simply as *axiomatic* in our research programs and focus our efforts on proposing theories to explain how this magical feat might be imagined actually to happen. (Since it *must* actually happen, there has to be some explanation of *how* it occurs!) On the other hand, it is fairly obvious that the eliminativist strategy adopted by the behaviorist and physicalist amounts to little more than outright capitulation to the rhetoric of scepticism. For, accepting that the sceptical critique is irrefutable, the only course left open to the eliminativist is to assume that children never do in fact bridge that ontological gap: children *never do* acquire a language, find out what their name is, learn the meanings of any words, or grasp the difference between true and false sentences. Accordingly, scientific research should leave those cultural fictions behind, along with Dennett's 'fatigues', on the garbage heap of folk-ontological confusion.

My position (as argued in Taylor, 1992, 1997) is that neither of these rhetorical strategies is satisfactory and, moreover, that the failure of modern human inquiry to tackle the sceptical problem head on has been a serious obstacle to scientific progress, with developmental linguistic research providing just one example. In the remainder of this paper, I will suggest a perspective from which a solution to the sceptical problem may be envisaged, one based on recognition of the reflexive character of language.

4. What is your name?

I will begin by considering an apparently trivial, yet still puzzling question, which is mostly ignored in the developmental research. When does a child learn her name?

The conventional answer is that a child learns her name sometime in the beginning or middle of her second year. However, there is some interesting evidence which indicates that this process moves slowly and that it in fact begins long before the second year. By using the well-known head-turn procedure, developmental psychologists such as Golinkoff and Hirsch-Pasek (1999) have determined that children respond differentially to their own names as early as 2 months old. That is, at the sound of her own name the child's face can be observed to light up. But it was only beginning around 6 months old that the children tested were observed to respond in a more distinctive fashion to the utterance of their name: turning and looking expectantly in the direction from which it was uttered. However, while the child's first *production* of her name is typically among the first words she utters, this rarely occurs any earlier than 12 months old and more usually somewhere in the middle of her second year (Shanker, 2001, p. 18).

So, when is it that a child has learned her name? Is it when she first responds automatically to hearing her name: that is, with her face brightening up? Or is it when she alters her focus of attention in response to its utterance? Or is it when she first produces the name? Or is it even later? For we might argue that for a child truly to have learned that, say, *Annie* is her name, she must be able to do more than look up every time when someone says "Annie". Many dogs will respond in this way when their name is produced—turning their heads and looking expectantly. Still, simply responding in an appropriate fashion to a particular vocal stimulus is hardly sufficient justification, is it, for the claim that a dog knows that *Rover* is *its name*? As many have pointed out—not the least of which was

Noam Chomsky in his (Chomsky, 1959) review of Skinner's *Verbal Behavior*—being conditioned to respond to a given vocalization is not the same thing as knowing that the vocalization is your name. After all, does a dog know what a name is? If not, then how can he know that *Rover* is his name? On the other hand, a parrot can be taught to pronounce its name. But does it know that it is saying *its name*? What evidence is there that any dog or parrot has acquired the reflexive metalinguistic knowledge of what a name is? None that I know of. We need to ask ourselves what sense it makes to say of a dog, a parrot, or a human infant that it knows that a given phonological form is its name but, none the less, does not yet know what a name is.

It would thus appear that acquiring the knowledge that all language-users eventually acquire—what their name is—is misconceived if it is theorized merely as a matter of coming to form an atomistic association between a certain set of sounds—say, [æ:ni]—and you. For what the adult knows in knowing that *Annie* is her name is very much more than this. In knowing that Annie is her name the adult knows what it is—in her linguistic community (or what the anthropologist Agar (1994) more aptly calls a "languaculture")—for *Annie* to be her name. In Anglophone languaculture this means knowing, for instance, that everyone has a name, that names often have more than one part, that your name identifies you (it declares 'who you are'), that a name cannot be easily changed, that typically when someone calls out your name they are seeking your attention, that putting your name on things is a means of identifying them as your own, and so on. In other languacultures knowing what a name is may involve knowing that saying an adult's name in public is impolite, or that you are not supposed to utter the name of a dead person, or that a name can only be given (or changed) in a special kind of ceremony, or that people have two names each of which is to be used exclusively in particular contexts, or that a person's name tells something about them (such as who their parents are or who their husband is), and so on. In other words, knowing *what a name is* is knowing what a name is *for us*. If you know what a name is, then you have learned what, in our languaculture, names are 'good for': what functions their use serves in our community, and how we value, choose, change, and generally treat them. That is, you know the *affordances* of names (Gibson, 1979). Furthermore, in attempting to explain the acquisition of names, we must not forget that, although children acquire personal names in every culture, the reflexive affordances of personal names vary substantially from culture to culture, especially when one looks beyond the all devouring behemoth called "Western culture". When these points are given the weight they deserve, it is very difficult to accept the metalinguistic concept of a name as some sort of acultural, autonomous (let alone, innate) universal.

Let me flesh this out a bit. If the little girl in question knows that *Annie* is her name, then in Anglophone languaculture we will expect her to be able to participate in reflexive exchanges about names that manifest that knowledge. In other words, she will be able to produce, or respond appropriately to, remarks like:

- "Hi, I'm Annie".
- "My name is Annie".
- "I'm called Annie".
- "Who are you?" ("Annie")
- "Tell us your name". ("Annie")
- "Is your name Annie?" ("Yes".)
- "Who is the girl called Annie?" ("It's me".)
- "Is there an Annie here?" ("Yes, me".)
- "The child by the name of Annie will have to leave now". ("OK".)

And if someone calls out "Annie", but Annie fails to answer, we will expect her to be able to make sense of their complaint that she didn't reply when—as we say—"her name was called".

If Annie is not able to participate competently in such reflexive exchanges, then it makes little sense to say of her that, all the same, she knows that *Annie* is her name. For whatever the sounds [æ:ni] are to her, she clearly does not treat them as what Anglophone culture calls a *name*.

It is worth pausing for a moment to ask ourselves what it would be like if there were *no* such reflexive exchanges as these I've just illustrated – in any languaculture. Among other things, it is hard to imagine how there could still be names – that is, how anyone could have a name. For how could a given sequence of sounds, such as [æ:ni], still be the *name* of a particular person if we had none of the reflexive practices of personal names? There would not be any way that those sounds could be *treated* as someone's name—that they could function in our interactions *as a name*—that is, if our culture had no metalinguistic expression like *name* and no reflexive practices in which this and related expressions (e.g., "[being] called") were used. A rose may be a rose by any other name, but a name is not a name unless we speak of it as such. It would seem, therefore, that an ineliminable part of learning that *Annie* is your name is learning its reflexive affordances, that is, learning how to participate competently (productively and responsively) in the kind of metadiscursive exchanges peculiar to our languaculture which treat *Annie* as your name.

Furthermore, it is clear that no dog or parrot could spontaneously produce or respond competently to the kind of reflexive remarks about their names that I have just instanced, but that any experienced speaker of English could do so with ease. It is no less clear that the infant who turns her head when her name is called will typically take many more months before she finally develops the abilities to participate competently in all such reflexive exchanges. As a component part of learning what her name is, a child must also, as Wittgenstein put it, learn what "post" names occupy in her culture's language games (Wittgenstein, 1953, Section 257). For if she cannot acquire this reflexive competence, then—like the four-month-old—her knowledge of her name will fundamentally be no different from that possessed by a dog or a parrot.

5. Metadiscourse in the zone of proximal development

Before considering the general implications of this illustrative example, it will help to reflect briefly on aspects of the theory of child development proposed by the Russian psychologist Lev Vygotsky and on their application in the recent work of two cognitive developmentalists influenced by him. Vygotsky's ideas were motivated by his recognition of a gap between the cognitive abilities that a child manifests in independent activity and the cognitive abilities that she manifests when aided by a competent adult. A child appears to possess a higher level of cognitive ability if she is supported in what she does by an adult, during which time she can accomplish cognitive tasks and solve problems which she is incapable of doing if working independently. This higher level of cognitive ability Vygotsky referred to as "the level of potential development". This is the level to which the child *will be able* to develop, but at the moment can only attain "under adult guidance or in collaboration with more capable peers" (Vygotsky, 1978, p. 86). The level at which she works *independently* Vygotsky called "the level of actual development". Thus, working independently, a given child may only be able to put together puzzle-problems of a certain level of difficulty. But, if the child is given assistance by a competent adult, she can solve puzzles of a much greater level of difficulty. This gap between a child's level of actual development and her level of potential

development Vygotsky termed "the zone of proximal development".

Secondly, Vygotsky took the child's development of
language skills to play a crucially transformative role in the
development of the child's other abilities. Vygotsky characterized a pre-linguistic child's ability to perform some action—
say, building a house out of plastic blocks—as a matter of
"practical mastery". But, he argued, once the child acquires
some linguistic skills, these skills take on

> a specific organizing function that penetrates the pro-
> cess and produces fundamentally new forms of behav-
> ior. (. . .) [A]s soon as speech and the use of signs are
> incorporated into any action, the action becomes trans-
> formed and organized along entirely new lines (Vygot-
> sky, 1978, p. 24).

Vygotsky also believed language to have this organiz-
ing function with regard to the development of the child's cognitive processes. Initially, speech functions as a component of
action but is functionally undifferentiated from the action itself
(cf. also Hickman, 1985). An intermediary stage may involve
the child's use of what Vygotsky called "egocentric speech":
that is, the child speaks aloud to herself as she performs a given
task: using speech as a guide to her actions. The final stage—
when speech has been "internalized", in Vygotsky's terms—
is when speech comes "to organize the child's thought"
(Vygotsky, 1978, p. 89).

Vygotsky's notion of the transformative role of language in cognitive development is extended by Annette
Karmiloff-Smith in her 1992 book *Beyond Modularity*. The
book's central concept is what she calls "representational redescription", a cognitive process which is crucial to the child's
development (Karmiloff-Smith, 1992, p. 190). Representational redescription transforms what is initially a form of

practical, behavioral mastery into explicit, manipulable knowledge. It operates by exploiting the procedural representations that the mind has already stored and reflexively redescribing them in a different representational format – for instance, in the format of a natural language (Karmiloff-Smith, 1992, p. 15). These new, explicit representations function as "meta-procedural operators" and can be consciously manipulated, used in a wide variety of contexts, and related to other reflexive representations, (Karmiloff-Smith, 1992, pp. 21–22) The crucial cognitive transformation brought about by representational redescription does not happen to the child all at once or to all of her cognitive abilities at the same time. Rather, as with Vygotsky's zone of proximal development, representational redescription is a gradual process, and one which affects different cognitive skills independently of others and at different times.

Karmiloff-Smith's example is that of a beginning pianist learning how to play a new piece on the piano. When a learner begins working on a new piece, he initially learns the notes in sequential chunks. After much practice, he will finally be able to play the piece from start to finish, more or less automatically. At this stage, the learner has acquired "behavioral mastery" of the task, which means that a given performance "is generated by procedural representations which are simply run off in their entirety" (Karmiloff-Smith, 1992, p. 16). The learner's performance is more or less automatic at this stage of behavioral mastery, and there is little flexibility or creative control possible. For instance, he is not yet able to interrupt his playing and take it up again in the middle of the piece – say, at the seventh bar. Nor is he able to create variations on a theme, change the sequential order of bars, or introduce insertions from other pieces. These sorts of abilities require more than the automatized procedural representations underlying behavioral mastery. They require representational redescription: the reorganization of those representations within a different representational format, in this case, musical notation. It is only then that

> knowledge of the different notes and chords becomes available as manipulable data. (. . .) The end result is representational flexibility and control, which allows for creativity. Also important is the fact that the earlier procedural capacity is not lost: for certain goals, the pianist can call on the automatic skill; for others, he or she calls on the more explicit representations that allow for flexibility and creativity. (Karmiloff-Smith, 1992, p. 16).

Karmiloff-Smith concludes that development and learning take what she terms "two complementary directions".

> On the one hand, they involve the gradual process of proceduralization (that is, rendering behavior more automatic and less accessible). On the other hand, they involve a process of "explicitation" and increasing accessibility (that is, representing explicitly information that is implicit in the procedural representations sustaining the behavior.) (Karmiloff-Smith, 1992, p. 17).

Most significantly, according to Karmiloff-Smith, these redescribed and reformatted representations allow the child to introduce *violations* to the behavioral routines she has acquired. This is what makes possible creative activities such as "pretend play, false belief, and the use of counterfactuals" (Karmiloff-Smith, 1992, p. 22). It is the reflexive redescription of the child's cognitive abilities which brings those abilities under her voluntary, context-independent control.

In addition to his views on the child's developmental stages and the transformative effect of language-learning on cognitive development, there is a third feature of Vygotsky's perspective taken up in Michael Tomasello's book *The Cultural Origins of Human Cognition* (1999). This is the Vygotskyan theme of the dialogic character of the child's "zone of proximal development". Tomasello cites his own studies and those of others (Ashley and Tomasello, 1998; Ratner and Hill, 1991; Foley and Ratner, 1997; Goudena, 1987; Kontos, 1983; Fernyhough, 1996), as evidence that, even for a child as young as 24 months, the child's interactional environment is permeated by various kinds of activities that are reflexively addressed to her contributions to the discourse. Tomasello groups these activities into three general types:

1. Disagreements (when an adult or peer explicitly disagrees with something the child has said).
2. Clarifications (when the child is asked to clarify what she has said or when a clarification is proposed by the other).
3. Didactic exchanges (when the adult or more capable peer "expresses a view on a view just expressed by the child" [Tomasello, 1999, p. 172]).

Tomasello argues that these metadiscursive activities have a constitutive role in the development of cognition (Tomasello, 1999, p. 173). In keeping with Vygotsky's account of how adult scaffolding helps the child perform to the level of potential development as well as with Karmiloff-Smith's views on the transformative nature of representational redescription, Tomasello affirms that, while these metadiscursive activities do not create basic skills *de novo*, they "turn basic cognitive skills into extremely complex and sophisticated cognitive skills" (Tomasello, 1999, p. 189). And, most importantly, their dialogic character leads the child to examine her own thinking reflexively, *from the perspective of her interlocutors*. Children "internalize the discourse in which adults instruct them or regulate their behavior. . .and this leads them to examine and reflect on their own thoughts and beliefs in the same way the adult has been doing" (Tomasello, 1999, pp. 190–191).

Tomasello argues that the reflexive representation which the child internalizes is fundamentally dialogical:

> [T]he child comprehends the adult instruction . . ., but she does so in relation to her own understanding— which requires a coordinating of the two perspectives. The cognitive representation that results, therefore, is a representation not just of the instructions but of the intersubjective dialogue. (Tomasello, 1999, p.193).

He adds, furthermore, that the internalized voice of the adult "is more than a bloodless point of view". On the contrary,

> [It] directs the child's cognition or behavior with more or less authority. Internalizing an instructional directive from an adult thus includes *both* a conceptual perspective and a moral injunction: 'You should look at it this way' (Tomasello, 1999, p. 194).

The result of this dialogical and normative form of representational redescription is that the child gradually develops the ability to self-monitor and self-regulate her own cognitive processes (Tomasello, 1999, p. 172). She is now able to produce independently (i.e., Vygotsky's level of actual development) behavior which she had previously only been able to perform under adult guidance (i.e., Vygotsky's level of potential development).

6. Bridging the gap: from behavioral mastery to reflexive understanding

How can these studies of cognitive transformation help us to address the ontological schizophrenia which plagues the study of language development? The child's initial command of communicational skills can be seen in terms of the Vygotskyan notion of practical or behavioral mastery. For illustrative purposes, let us imagine a child who can be observed to do the following (albeit not all at the same time).

- The child turns her head when the sounds of her name are pronounced. (However, she does not yet tell people that her name is Annie or reply with her name when asked "What's your name?". And she does not yet respond appropriately when someone asks "Who is called 'Annie' here?" or "Will the girl named 'Annie' please raise her hand".)
- She says "shoe" when looking at a shoe. (However, she doesn't yet know what to say if asked "What's this thing called?" or "Do you mean my shoe or your shoe?" Nor does she respond appropriately when her parent says "No, not 'shoe'; it's a sock" or (pointing at a shoe) asks "Is this what you are talking about?" or "Yes. What do you want to say about the shoe?" She does not yet know how to make appropriate contributions to reflexive exchanges about the word or its use.)
- When talking about pins and pens, her utterances sometimes include the expressions [pɪn] and [pɜn]. (However, she cannot yet participate competently in reflexive exchanges about the expressions being "different words" or about the expressions having "different meanings". She doesn't know how to make an appropriate response to "Did you say [pɪn] or [pɜn]?".)

- She says "Dog there" when she hears the family dog out-side the door. (However, she is not yet familiar with the ordinary metadiscursive methods by which such an asser-tion may be queried or supported, its reference explained ("Which dog?" or "Where?"), its purpose or contextual rel-evance clarified ("So? Why are you saying this?"), or its truth justified ("No it's not, is it?"). She has not yet mas-tered the reflexive affordances of such an assertion.)
- Some of her utterances are fully grammatical; others are grammatically incomplete or incorrect. (However, she does not yet know how to participate—productively or re-sponsively—in normative metadiscourse about how some-thing *should* be said.)
- She says the neighbors "don't speak English", that she can't "understand" them, and that they "speak Swahili". (However, she cannot yet participate competently in meta-discursive exchanges about speaking (or not speaking) a given language or understanding (or not understanding) a language. Nor do her contributions or responses to meta-discourse about languages yet manifest understanding of what a language is or what it means to speak or understand a given language.)

Within her familiar interactional environments, the child expresses her behavioral mastery of these and many other communicational skills. Crucially, it is here, in Vygot-sky's "zone of proximal development", that her verbal behav-ior—her responsive behavior no less importantly than the pro-ductive—becomes an explicit topic of reflexive attention. Her interactional environment is permeated by metadiscursive feedback addressed to her verbal behavior, as well as to the verbal behavior of co-present others. She hears metalinguistic labels, repair initiations, explicit correction and modeling, re-casts and offers, normative and evaluative assessments of what she or someone else has said, metacommunicational directives, explanations of meaning and reference, and so on (Aukrust, 2001, 2004; Becker, 1994; Blum-Kulka and Snow, 2004; Demetras et al., 1986; Dunn, 1988; Kontos, 1983; Levy, 1999; Quasthoff, 1995; Stude, 2007; Tomasello, 1999).

Because of the inherently reflexive nature of turn sequencing in dialogue (Wootton, 1997), the child also observes less explicit forms of linguistic reflexivity. Each next turn, by means of its sequential relevance to the prior turn, typically manifests some reflexive assessment of the latter. While some of these interpretations and inferences are made the explicit topics of reflexive remarks, many are not. For instance, the child witnesses manifestations—both verbal and nonverbal—of the interpretations and inferential consequences which her interlocutors draw from the things she says; and she sees her interlocutors' *own* responses to the interpretations and inferential consequences which she draws from the utterances that they produce. In sum, the dialogic character of the child's interactional environment insures that

1. The child is constantly presented with reflexive (often normative) feedback, explicit and implicit, about her own and others' linguistic behavior.
2. She is herself called upon to produce appropriate reflexive responses, explicit and implicit, to what others say (including to what they say in next-turn position following something that she has said).

The reflexive character of the child's zone of proximal development has a transformative effect on her linguistic abilities. With the guiding, co-regulating support of her caregivers, she acquires a greater and greater command of the reflexive aspects of dialogic interaction. Accordingly, she begins to use her communicational skills—and respond to the communicational acts of others—with a greater awareness of their reflexive affordances. A good example of this kind of guided support can be found in the formatted language games discussed in Bruner (1983) and in the studies stimulated by this groundbreaking book (e.g., Bruner, 1985). It is when acting with the assistance of these adult-controlled interactional scaffolds—such as Bruner's "name game"—that the child is able to perform to what Vygotsky called her "level of potential development": that is, *beyond the level of actual development reflected in the skills she deploys in independent activity*. Aided by the reflexive support of adult prompts, modeling, recasts, third-turn repairs, and the more-or-less routinized patterning of the exchanges, the child begins, for example, to respond more competently to uses of her name than by the mere turning of her head. She starts to respond "Annie" when an adult asks "What's your name?" And she says "Yes" when asked "Is your name Annie?" She raises her hand if an adult asks "Is there anyone called Annie here?" And so on. The child is coming to grasp, that is, what Wittgenstein called the "grammar" of names in her languaculture (Wittgenstein, 1953, Sections 29, 199, 371). Gradually, she is able to make increasingly independent contributions—productive as well as responsive—to metadiscursive exchanges involving the use of her name. In other words, she is learning what it means that *Annie* is her name; she is becoming able to make the kind of independent contributions to reflexive exchanges involving her name that Anglophone languaculture takes to be criterial for determining whether someone—a child or an ape or a parrot—knows that N is their name. It is at this point that we may say that the child's knowledge of her name has progressed from Vygotsky's level of potential development to the—independently controlled and reflexively competent—level of actual development. Or, from a Saussurean perspective, it could be said that the child now sees the sounds of her name from the "emic" viewpoint, the viewpoint from which language *substance* is transformed into language *form*.

The cognitive scientist or philosopher might make use of another conventional way of characterizing the kind of transformation that occurs when the child moves from the behavioral mastery of particular verbal skills to the independent command of their reflexive affordances. The child would be said to be developing metalinguistic *concepts*: the concept of a name, the concept of talking 'about' something, the concept of a word having a particular meaning, the concept of being (or not being) understood, the concept of speaking a particular language, the concept of word-identity, the concept of saying something correctly (or incorrectly), and the concept of saying something true (or false). Using this register of scientific meta-discourse, we could say that in the zone of proximal development the child acquires the metalinguistic concepts to go along with, and representationally redescribe, her initial behavioral mastery of the verbal phenomena in question.

It is at this stage that the child might also be said to experience language in the way that the immanence theorist takes her to have done from the very start (and the way that the sceptical eliminativist takes her never to achieve). Gradually, parts of her behavioral mastery of verbal phenomena have become reflexively enculturated: that is, by means of the particular patterns of reflexive discourse characteristic of her family, her neighborhood, her community, and her cultural form of life. In other words, in contrast to John Searle's above-quoted claim that language is self-identifying, the proposal put forward here is that the child does not begin with forms of behavior that are, *sui generis*, "already language" (Searle, 1995, p. 73). On the contrary, a child's name does not enter her verbal repertoire *as a name*. A child's "request" does not begin with the properties that our linguistic commonsense attributes to a request (cf. Taylor and Shanker, 2003). Nor does the meaning of a given word (e.g., *shoe*) or of a true statement (e.g., "Dog there") begin for the child with the properties that competent speakers take word-meanings and true sentences to have. Language does not begin developmentally *as language*. That is, the child's "language" does not emerge in her behavioral repertoire already in possession of those properties that the competent speakers of the community assume language to have: those very properties that commonsense insists language possesses (and which thus become the fodder for language theorizing). Language does not begin like that; but, *contra* the sceptic, that is how it ends up.

When considering the transformative role of metadiscourse in the child's zone of proximal development, we must keep at the very forefront of our minds an important aspect that I do not have the space to give sufficient attention to here (and which is dangerously obscured by my use of Anglophone examples throughout this essay). *The types of reflexive feedback that the child receives in her interactional environment vary in myriad and non-generalizable ways from culture to culture.* In other words, the reflexive enculturation which a child's linguistic competence undergoes is as variable as are the forms of folk metadiscourse displayed in languacultures around the world (Cf., among others, Blum, 1997; Blum-Kulka and Sheffer, 1993; Bublitz and Hubler, 2007; Grey and Fiering, 2000; Keeler, 2008; Kuipers, 2008; Lillard, 1997, 1998; Lucy, 1993; Rumsey, 1990; Shanker, 2001; Sherzer, 1983; Silverstein, 1985, 1993; Stross, 1974; Verschueren, 1985). This is crucially important because it means that the properties that language comes to possess for the mature speaker–hearer are not the same from culture to culture. To use the expression (if not the intention) of Searle (1995), the metadiscursive "construction" of language is culturally variable. While basic human universals may influence the child's initial behavioral mastery of linguistic phenomena, it is the cultural specificity of folk metadiscourse which transforms that initial mastery into the adult competence expressed in that particular culture's commonsense metadiscourse. We should not assume that the reflexive enculturation of language is a matter of species universality nor for that matter, of social consensus, historical uniformity, or even intra-cultural homogeneity.

7. Conclusion: where language comes from

This, then, is the solution I propose to the sceptical problem raised earlier. It is by reflexive enculturation that the child crosses the categorial gap from the behavioral and physical properties of linguistic development to those properties whose cultural reality is reflected in the metalinguistic "truisms" of commonsense. Moreover, these are the very properties which, if discarded under the exigencies of sceptical eliminativism, would leave a phenomenon of language which is *nothing like we experience or know it to be*—and on whose properties we must and do rely in the moment-to-moment activities of our daily communicational lives.

The proposal I have put forward does not imply that there is no complex behavioral and neurological mastery to be acquired by the child. Nor, I should stress, does it rule out the possibility of nativist explanations of the development of crucial parts of that mastery – whether explanations of the formal-autonomist kind, such as that envisaged by generative minimalists, or of the cognitive-functionalist kind as advocated by developmentalists such as Tomasello. It does not rule out such nativist explanations; *nor however does it make them necessary*. However, although there is still room for a base-level, minimal set of innate predispositions which guide the child's development of various kinds of behavioral mastery, the view argued for here most definitely does not represent the "emic" transformation that then occurs as anything like the setting of pre-defined parametric switches or the recognition of inherent properties of communicational phenomena.

On the contrary, the view I am proposing takes the real, distinctive properties of language—or, to put it differently, *the linguistic identity of language*—to be the result of the processes of reflexive enculturation. By means of reflexive enculturation, language is transformed from a matter of behavioral mastery—and the neurological and physiological processes that enable that mastery—into a phenomenon of an entirely different categorial type. Now—in Anglophone languaculture, at least—we have meanings; now we have true and false sentences; now we have word identity; now we have personal names; now we have particular languages, dialects, and accents; now we have referring to and "talking about" this thing or that event; now we have what you "should" say and how it "is" pronounced and what it "really" means; now we have stating, lying, ordering, complaining, explaining, justifying, teasing, and asking. Now we have language.[1]

Acknowledgements

I am deeply grateful to my friend and colleague John Joseph, without whose support and encouragement this article would never have been written. Institutional and financial support for the research leading to and the writing of this article was provided, most generously, by The Leverhulme Trust, The

---

[1] Furthermore, now we have linguistics. For the foundations of every major school of linguistic theory depend on native judgments of these kinds. ("This is the same word as that"; "W has the same meaning as X"; "This sentence is false"; "She is speaking Danish; he is speaking Swedish"; "He is referring to the last king of France"; "'The hamster me bit' is incorect"; etc.) Therefore, not only is the child's maturing metadiscursive competence where language-as-we-know-it comes from. It is also where linguistics-as-we-know-it comes from – albeit with radically different ontological and epistemological foundations from those which have always hitherto been assumed. But this is a topic for another day.

National Humanities Center (Delmas Fellowship), The College of William and Mary, and the Institute of Advanced Studies in the Humanities (University of Edinburgh).

References

Agar, M., 1994. *Language Shock: Understanding the Culture of Conversation*. William Morrow, New York.

Ashley, J., Tomasello, M., 1998. "Cooperative problem solving and teaching in preschoolers." *Social Development* 17, 143–163.

Aukrust, V.G., 2001. "Talk-focused talk in preschools – culturally formed socialization for talk?" *First Language* 21, 57–82.

Aukrust, V.G., 2004. "Talk about talk with young children: pragmatic socialization in two communities in Norway and the US." *Journal of Child Language* 31, 177–201.

Becker, J.A., 1994. "Pragmatic socialization: parental input to preschoolers." *Discourse Processes* 17, 131–148.

Blum, S., 1997. "Naming practices and the power of words in China." *Language in Society* 26, 357–379.

Blum-Kulka, S., Sheffer, H., 1993. "The metapragmatic discourse of American–Israeli families at dinner." In: Kasper, G., Blum-Kulka, S. (Eds.), *Interlanguage Pragmatics*. Oxford University Press, New York, pp. 196–223.

Blum-Kulka, S., Snow, C.E. (Eds.), 2004. *Talking to Adults: The Contribution of Multiparty Discourse to Language Acquisition*. Lawrence Erlbaum, Mahwah.

Bruner, J., 1983. *Child's Talk: Learning to Use Language*. Oxford University Press, Oxford.

Bruner, J., 1985. "The role of interaction formats in language acquisition." In: Forgas, J. (Ed.), *Language and Social Situations*. Springer, New York.

Bublitz, W., Hubler, A. (Eds.), 2007. *Metapragmatics in Use*. Benjamins, Amsterdam.

Chomsky, N., 1959. "Review of B.F. Skinner: Verbal behavior." *Language* 35, 26–58.

Churchland, P., 1991. "Folk psychology and the explanation of human behaviour." In: Greenwood, J. (Ed.), *The Future of Folk Psychology*. Cambridge University Press, Cambridge.

Demetras, M., Post, K., Snow, D., 1986. "Feedback to first language learners: the role of repetitions and clarification questions." *Journal of Child Language* 13, 275–292.

Dennett, D., 1981. *Brainstorms*. MIT Press, Cambridge, MA.

Dunn, J., 1988. *The Beginnings of Social Understanding*. Blackwell, Oxford.

Fernyhough, C., 1996. "The dialogic mind: a dialogic approach to the higher mental functions." *New Ideas in Psychology* 14, 47–62.

Foley, M., Ratner, H., 1997. "Children's recording in memory for collaboration: a way of learning from others." *Cognitive Development* 13, 91–108.

Gibson, J.J., 1979. *The Ecological Approach to Visual Perception*. Houghton Mifflin, Boston.

Golinkoff, R., Hirsch-Pasek, K., 1999. *How Babies Talk*. Dutton, New York.

Goudena, P., 1987. "The social nature of private speech of preschoolers during problem solving." *International Journal of Behavioral Development* 10, 187–206.

Grey, E., Fiering, N. (Eds.), 2000. *The Language Encounter in the Americas: 1492–1800*. Berghahn Books, New York.

Hickman, M., 1985. "Metapragmatics in child language." In: Mertz, E., Permentier, R.J. (Eds.), *Semiotic Mediation: Sociocultural and Psychological Perspectives.* Academic Press, New York.

Karmiloff-Smith, A., 1992. *Beyond Modularity: A Developmental Perspective on Cognitive Science.* MIT Press, Cambridge (MA).

Keeler, L., 2008. "Linguistic reconstruction and the construction of nationalist-era Chinese linguistics." *Language & Communication* 28, 344–361.

Kontos, S., 1983. "Adult-child interaction and the origins of metacognition." *Journal of Educational Research* 77, 43–54.

Kuipers, J., 2008. "Named speech registers and the inscription of locality in the Dutch East Indies." *Language & Communication* 28, 308–321.

Levy, Y., 1999. "Early metalinguistic competence: speech monitoring and repair behavior." *Developmental Psychology* 35, 822–834.

Lillard, A., 1997. "Other folks' theories of mind and behavior." *Psychological Science* 8, 268–274.

Lillard, A., 1998. "Ethnopsychologies: cultural variations in theories of mind." *Psychological Bulletin* 23, 3–32.

Lucy, J., 1993. "Metapragmatic presentationals: reporting speech with quotatives in Yucatec Maya." In: Lucy, J. (Ed.), *Reflexive Language.* Cambridge University Press, Cambridge.

Macnamara, J.T., 1982. *Names for Things.* MIT Press, Cambridge, MA.

Pinker, S., 1994. *The Language Instinct.* Morrow, New York.

Quasthoff, U.M., 1995. "The ontogenetic aspect of orality: towards the interactive constitution of linguistic development." In: Quasthoff, U.M. (Ed.), *Aspects of*

Oral Communication. Mouton de Gruyter, Berlin, pp. 256–274.

Ratner, H., Hill, L., 1991. "Regulation and representation in the development of children's memory." Paper presented to the Society for Research in Child Development, Seattle.

Rumsey, A., 1990. "Wording, meaning and linguistic ideol ogy." *American Anthropologist* 92, 346–361.

Sahlins, M., 1977. *Culture and Practical Reason*. University of Chicago Press, Chicago.

Searle, J., 1995. *The Construction of Social Reality*. Free Press, New York.

Shanker, S., 2001. "What children know when they know what a name means." *Current Anthropology* 42 (4).

Sherzer, J., 1983. *Kuna Ways of Speaking*. University of Texas Press, Austin.

Shwe, H., Markman, E., 1999. "Young children's apprecia- tion of the mental impact of their communicative sig- nals." In: Slater, A., Muir, D. (Eds.), *The Blackwell Reader in Developmental Psychology*. Blackwell, Ox- ford.

Silverstein, M., 1985. "The culture of language in Chinookan narrative texts, or, on saying that . . . in Chinook." In: Nichols, J., Woodbury, A. (Eds.), *Grammar Inside and Outside the Clause*. Cambridge University Press, Cambridge.

Silverstein, M., 1993. "Metapragmatic discourse and meta- pragmatic function." In: Lucy, J. (Ed.), *Reflexive Lan- guage*. Cambridge University Press, Cambridge.

Stich, S., 1983. *From Folk Psychology to Cognitive Science*. MIT Press, Cambridge (MA).

Stross, B., 1974. "Speaking of speaking: Tenejapa Tzeltal metalinguistics." In: Baumann, R. (Ed.), *Explorations in the Ethnography of Speaking.* Cambridge University Press, Cambridge.

Stude, J., 2007. "The acquisition of metapragmatic abilities in preschool children." In: Bublitz, W., Hubler, A. (Eds.), *Metapragmatics in Use.* Benjamins, Amsterdam, pp. 199–220.

Taylor, T.J., 1992. *Mutual Misunderstanding: Scepticism and the Theorizing of Language and Interpretation.* Duke University Press, Durham (NC).

Taylor, T.J., 1997. *Theorizing Language: Analysis, Normativity, Rhetoric, History.* Pergamon Press, Oxford.

Taylor, T.J., Shanker, S., 2003. "Rethinking language acquisition: what children learn." In: Davis, H., Taylor, T.J. (Eds.), *Rethinking Linguistics.* Routledge, London.

Tomasello, M., 1999. *The Cultural Origins of Human Cognition.* Harvard University Press, Cambridge (MA).

Verschueren, J., 1985. *What People Say They Do With Words.* Ablex, Norwood (NJ).

Vygotsky, L.S., 1978. *Mind in Society.* Harvard University Press, Cambridge (MA).

Watson, J., 1913. "Psychology as the behaviorist views it." *Psychological Review* 20, 158–177.

Watson, J., 1924. *Behaviorism.* University of Chicago Press, Chicago.

Wierzbicka, A., 2001. "Comments." *Current Anthropology* 42(4), 506–507.

Wittgenstein, L., 1953. *Philosophical Investigations.* Blackwell, Oxford.

Wootton, A.J., 1997. *Interaction and the Development of Mind.* Cambridge University Press, Cambridge.

III

Language development
and the integrationist

Abstract

Despite the growing body of integrationist literature on the study of language and on a wide range of language-related fields of inquiry, there is as yet no integrationist investigation of the field of language acquisition. This paper argues for the need for an integrationist study of what children learn about language and of how they learn it. What children come to know about language—its forms, content, and properties, its powers and its uses—is largely a culturally defined product of commonplace metadiscursive practices, in much the same way as what children come to know about other sociocultural, moral, and psychological domains is an outcome of their increasingly competent participation within the discursive practices of their developmental environment.

1. Introduction

Since his first publications in linguistics in the 1970s, Roy Harris has been one of the most prolific, insightful, and original writers on language and on a wide variety of academic disciplines that have overlapping interests with the study of language. His published works and lectures have brought about a fundamental and far-reaching tectonic shift, if still not fully completed, in intellectual discourse on language. Supplementing his own voluminous writings, those of Harris' fellow integrationists have successfully extended the integrationist perspective to even more fields of inquiry. There are now authoritative integrationist critiques of the study of science, art, history, the law, psychology, literary style, writing, translation, epistemology, and logic, as well as a small library of works on the various components of language itself. However, a surprising anomaly is the absence—to my knowledge—of an integrationist investigation of child language development (a.k.a. language acquisition).

This is a curious omission. For in recent decades, a central place in Western linguistic theorizing has been given to questions about the acquisition of a child's first language. A prime motivation for the priority given to language-developmental questions has been the work of Noam Chomsky and the generative school of linguistic theory, which grounds its postulation of a uniquely human, innate language faculty in what is called the argument from the "poverty of experience". One crucial implication of generativist theory is the meta-theoretical principle that any claim about some item of linguistic knowledge—in plain words, about something which the competent language user knows—must be supported by a plausible argument about how children do, or at least could, acquire that knowledge. According to this meta-theoretical principle, if that knowledge cannot be shown to be acquirable by means of the child's experience, then either it must be a component of the postulated innate language faculty—and to merit this status it must satisfy a further set of meta-theoretical criteria—or it must not in fact be a bona fide item of linguistic knowledge at all. *If it cannot be explained how human children could acquire that knowledge, then the linguist should accept that it could not possibly be something that adult language-users know.* This reasoning is one of the most important means by which generative linguists—and Chomsky as the authoritative leader of the school—impose rhetorical control over the admission of linguists' claims about linguistic knowledge. A given item of knowledge K can only be accepted as a part of the competent speaker-hearer's linguistic knowledge if there is a plausible account of how children could acquire K by means of ordinary experiential learning (i.e., despite the "poverty of experience") or if there is an acceptable argument (according to the norms of the latest version of generativist meta-theory) for the attribution of K to the domain of the innate language faculty. Significantly, this meta-theoretical requirement has been widely accepted by language theorists in recent decades and not only by adherents to generativism. The fact that neither Harris nor any other integrationist has addressed the issue of how children develop language risks being seen as a rhetorical weakness in the integrationist approach. Perhaps, so the critics of integrationism would say, the reason no developmental wing exists in the integrationist architecture is that the abilities and knowledge which integrationists attribute to competent, adult language-users could not ever be acquired by children—a conclusion which yields the corollary that the attribution of these abilities and knowledge to competent adult language users is at best a misrepresentation and, more probably, false.

At the very least, integrationism ought to develop a response to the meta-theoretical argument which ties the justification of theoretical claims about linguistic knowledge and abilities to arguments about how—or even whether—children are able to acquire those abilities and knowledge. Even better, in my view, would be to incorporate an account of language development into the growing body of integrationist theory. It is worth noting that, in facing this challenge, the integrationist has the example of Wittgenstein before him, a philosopher of language whose views run parallel to integrationism in more places and for greater distances than any other. Wittgenstein, not unlike several integrationist writers, has often been misinterpreted as being a covert behaviorist. However, Wittgenstein was aware of this criticism (e.g., Wittgenstein, 2009, sec. 307) and so, given his goal to avoid the Scylla and Charybdis of psychologistic and behaviorist approaches, framed substantial parts of his discussions of language against a developmental backdrop. The integrationist, I would suggest, needs to adopt an analogous rhetorical strategy, even if the theoretical goals and arguments of integrationism differ from those of Wittgenstein. The work of Harris and other integrationists has similarly been criticized for its purported crypto-behaviorism; and the absence of a sustained and convincing response to this criticism runs the risk of being perceived as an admission of vulnerability to that criticism.

There is still another reason why integrationism should consider devoting more discussion to language development. To date, the loudest volleys of integrationist discourse have been aimed at the foundational assumptions and theoretical consequences of (what the integrationist calls) "segregational" perspectives on language. Segregational linguistics views signs, meanings, and whole languages to exist and possess properties independently of particular circumstances of use. It would seem that integrationism cannot secure its foothold in contemporary thought until it has put to rout its arch-rival, segregationism. This may or may not be accurate as a matter of rhetorical strategy; but what is most significant in the current context is that segregationist approaches currently reign absolutely supreme in the academic study of language development. If the segregationist lion is to be vanquished, he must be sought and defeated in his lair.

It is not my goal in this paper to propose an integrationist account of language development, or even to sketch the outlines of one. My primary goal has been simply to explain why there is a need for the integrationist approach founded by Roy Harris to articulate an account of how children learn language. I believe that such an account would have great potential for our understanding of human language and human learning. However, in addition to this primary goal, I want to draw attention to an important feature of language development to which I believe an integrationist theory—indeed, any satisfactory account of language development—needs to accord a central role.

The following conversation between an adult and a two-year-old girl was reported in an article published in 1990 by C. Peterson:

> Child: He bite my leg.
> Adult: What?
> Child: Duck bite my leg
> Adult: The dog bit your leg. Oh, oh, the duck. Oh boy!
> Child: Me go in the water.
> Adult: You went in the water?
> Child: Yeah. My leg.

There is nothing surprising about this conversation. It is quite typical of a verbal exchange involving a child learning English in his or her third year of life. Yet, viewed from the dominant, segregational perspective in linguistics, it is vastly more complex than one might think. Indeed, from that perspective, its achievement appears to be nothing short of miraculous. The epistemic properties that the child's utterances are said to reveal are so formidably complex and abstract that, so the argument goes, only the existence of innate structures, processes, or faculties could explain how the child ever was able to acquire them.

According to the most generic version of segregational linguistics, the child must possess a substantial volume of linguistic knowledge in order to be able to produce these remarks and engage competently in a conversation of this degree of sophistication. The following list contains a sample selection of some of the items of which this knowledge is comprised. The items in this list are here phrased in what is intended to be minimally technical and model-neutral language; that is, it is given in the generic phraseology of traditional grammatical and semantic description, which, although generally homologous with, is not specific to the requirements of any particular linguistic model. It should be clear that, expressed in such generic, non-technical terms, the items listed still serve adequately as *samples* of the types of knowledge which segregational linguistic theories would attribute to a child who is able to participate competently in the conversation quoted above. Indeed, this is my only goal in presenting this list. For the purposes of the following discussion, I have used bold type to foreground the linguistic character of the items of knowledge which, in each case, are being attributed to the child.

1. The word *duck* **means** a particular kind of animal characterized by certain recognizable features.
2. In the child's second remark, the child's first **word** —"duck"—**refers** to a particular instance of this animal—one which the child has encountered on an occasion in the past.

3. Each of the child's remarks **asserts a proposition** about this past occasion: that is, the child is asserting that each of her remarks **expresses a meaning which is true of** the events that occurred at that time.

4. The child's utterance "he" in the first sentence also **refers** to the animal in question.

5. The English word *bite* **means** a particular action in volving the opening and closing of a mouth by agent A in contact with an object O.

6. The child's **uses of the English word** *bite* in the first and third remarks refer to an actual instance of this action which occurred on the past occasion.

7. The child's first two utterances **represent** the duck **as standing in an agent-action relationship** to this action of biting.

8. The child's first two utterances **represent** a leg as **standing in an action-object relationship** to the action of biting.

9. The remark "my leg" in the child's first, second, and fourth utterances all **refer** to the same object (i.e., the same leg) featuring in the event reported.

10. The remark "my leg" **signifies** that the leg in question is one of the child's legs.

11. The child's remark "me go in the water" **refers to** the same past occasion on which occurred the biting reported by the child.

12. The child's remark "me go in the water" **is intended to indicate** the contextual circumstances in which occurred the action of biting.

13. The child's remark "Yeah" **expresses her understanding** of the adult's immediately preceding remark **as a particular type of question,**

namely, what linguists call "Yes-No questions".

14. The child's remark "Yeah" **expresses her under
    standing of and agreement with** the assertion
    which is **pragmatically implied** by the adult's
    immediately preceding question, namely, that
    the child had gone into the water at the time that
    the biting occurred.

15. The child's final remark, "My leg", **indexes** and
    **specifies the reference of "me" in her previ-
    ous remark**, "Me go in the water".

Although it is long and quite linguistically sophisticated, this list is only a very partial sample of the items of linguistic knowledge which the dominant perspective in linguistics would claim that this 2-year-old child possesses and indeed draws on in producing her contributions to this exchange.
That is, she must, apparently, already know these things, since
she is manifestly able to participate quite competently in this
real-life conversational snippet. If she did *not know* these
things, so the argument goes, then she would *not be able* to
participate as competently in this conversation as she does.
Moreover, we may assume that the child engages in many such
conversational exchanges each day. If, therefore, we were to
draw a complete list of all such items of linguistic knowledge
which a child is taken *necessarily* to possess in order to be able
to communicate as she does throughout the day, then that list
would obviously be very much longer.

At the same time, it is important to recognize that this
list of particular items of linguistic knowledge carries the implication that the child also possesses more general items of
linguistic knowledge. The child must know, for instance, not
merely that the word *duck* means a particular kind of animal
but, more generally, what a word is and what it is to mean

something. For how could she not know what a word is or what it is to mean something *and yet still know that a given word means such-and-such*? In other words, in addition to the items listed above, the child must also know

> i. what it is for a word to mean something,
> ii. what it is to refer to something,
> iii. what it is for an utterance to be true of some event,
> iv. what it is for an utterance to assert a proposition,
> v. what it is to understand and to express one's understanding of an utterance,
> vi. what it is for an utterance to pragmatically imply a meaning,
> vii. what it is to intend to express a meaning,
> viii. what a question is.

Naturally, few if any linguistic theorists would claim that the child has explicit, verbal knowledge of such conceptually sophisticated and technical information as that listed in i–viii. However, the dominant perspective in linguistics is necessarily committed to the claim that the child has at least tacit knowledge of such general metalinguistic properties, knowledge that any given linguistic theory would explicitly formulate according to its own terminological conventions.

It is therefore quite understandable that, within the dominant segregational paradigm in linguistics, the overarching question which determines the research programs investigating child language development is this: *How can children as young as two years old come to possess such a vast and conceptually sophisticated inventory of knowledge as that exemplified by 1–15 and, by implication, i–viii?* And yet they must ... somehow. For otherwise they would apparently be unable to participate as competently as does the child in the verbal exchange quoted above? For the limited purposes of the discussion in this paper, segregational approaches to this question may be loosely grouped into two general types. One of these, which we may call "cognitive interactionism," holds that the child acquires the kind of knowledge listed in 1–15 and i–viii gradually, item by item, with the assistance of innate cognitive structures and capacities, along with the "scaffolding" support of the child's socio-interactional environment. The major research issues for the cognitive interactionist approach thus concern the specific nature of these innate cognitive structures and capacities as well as the means by which, in interaction with the child's developmental environment, these yield the kind of linguistic knowledge itemized in 1–15 and i–viii. The other major theoretical approach is that of linguistic nativism. Linguistic nativists take the most important features of the child's linguistic knowledge to be the product of her innate language faculty: a genetic endowment unique to the human species. Nativists claim that there really is only one very general item of knowledge which a child has to learn from experience: namely, *which* language is spoken in her developmental environment. For once this is known, the particular items of knowledge required to speak and understand that language are automatically acquired by means of the child's language faculty. The major research issue for the linguistic nativist is thus one of identifying the specific properties of this innate faculty.

There are, of course, crucially important differences between these two types of approach to the study of language development. It is nonetheless essential to recognize that they share the assumption that, in order to be able to participate competently in verbal exchanges equal to and eventually surpassing the sophistication of the conversation quoted above, children require some means of acquiring a theory-specific version of the kind of items of linguistic knowledge listed in

1–15 and i–viii. The question of how such linguistic knowledge is acquired is therefore a shared theoretical goal for both general types of approach and so has naturally become the overarching question determining the research programs in modern approaches to the study of language development. Given the principles of integrational linguistics, as spelled out in Harris' works and in the works of other integrationists, we may safely say that an integrationist approach to language development would reject this overarching question. An integrationist approach would also reject the theoretical postulation of innate faculties, structures, and abilities which has characterized the approaches of cognitive interactionism and nativism. Beyond this, however, the specific properties of an integrationist approach to language development have not yet been made clear.

The suggestion put forward in this paper (and discussed in more detail elsewhere: cf. Taylor, 1997, 2000, 2010; Taylor and Shanker, 2003) is that any satisfactory approach to child language development must give due attention to the reflexive—in particular, the metadiscursive—nature of the child's developing linguistic knowledge. What we come to know of language—its forms, content, and properties, its powers and uses—is largely a culturally defined construct of our commonplace metadiscursive practices, in much the same way as is what we take ourselves to know about other sociocultural, moral, and psychological domains. Our acquisition of linguistic knowledge, in other words, is informed by our developing ability to participate (receptively as well as productively) in the metadiscursive practices of our communicational community. For instance, an adult language-user will characteristically refer to himself as a "speaker of English" or of some other "language". In the case of the "speaker of English", he will typically speak of a "word" as possessing what he calls a "meaning", of two people who are "talking to each other" as

"understanding" or "not understanding" what the other "says",
and of the vocal sounds speakers produce as being particular
"words" or "sentences" and as having particular powers: such
as "being about", "describing", and "being true (or false)" of a
given object, event, or situation. We would naturally expect to
hear a member of Anglophone languaculture characterize the
sequence of sounds [dʌk], produced by the child in the conversation above, as "meaning" something—indeed, as having the
particular meaning which belongs to that sequence of sounds
as a word of "the English language". And we would expect
him to characterize the adult's third remark in the conversation—"You went in the water?"—as a "request" for the child
to confirm the adult's expressed "understanding" of her previous remark ("Me go in the water"). Children or adults who
were not able to participate competently in ordinary metadiscursive practices incorporating these and many other such
reflexive remarks would not typically be taken to "know English" or to "know what the meaning of *duck* is" or to "know
what so-and-so said": that is, competent adult speakers of English would not typically speak of them in such metalinguistic
terms. Coming to master Anglophone ways of talking about
language is internally related to the child's developing mastery
of what, in the professional metadiscourse of linguists, is typically referred to as 'knowledge of the English language'.

There would be many important consequences for an
approach to the study of language development which gave
due attention to the reflexive character of language. I will only
mention two here. First, recognition of the reflexive character
of language would lead developmental theorists to refrain
from the mistake of taking the properties and powers which,
in such metadiscursive practices, are *attributed* to language
(that is to say, to language systems and forms, their speakers,
and the circumstances of language use) to be indicative of the
properties and powers *possessed* by language itself (language

systems and forms, their speakers, and the circumstances of language use). The reflexive construction of language, a product of the child's initiation into everyday metadiscursive routines, has too often led language theorists to see the properties and powers with which we commonly characterize verbal activity as inhering in the very phenomena of language itself: whether in the linguistic units employed (words, sentences, prosodic patterns, etc.), in the language users' minds or brains, or in their verbal acts. Consequently, when language developmentalists study the child's acquisition of the knowledge required to become a competent language user, they are naturally inclined to assume that the knowledge in question is knowledge of these inherent properties and powers of language. Yet, as the sample lists 1–15 and i–viii suggest, the items of knowledge which the child would therefore need to acquire would have to be forbiddingly complex and numerous. Language-learning thus comes to be portrayed by the dominant segregational approaches as a matter of acquiring knowledge of potentially infinite and unlearnable dimensions, a picture which in turn leads those approaches into the theoretical cul-de-sac from which the only escape is to propose the kinds of innate faculties, structures, abilities, and processes which characterize current linguistic-developmental theories.

Second, giving due attention to the reflexive character of language would encourage the developmentalist to look more closely at the child's experience of and growing ability to participate in metadiscursive practices. For what language becomes for the child is something constructed gradually by means of the metadiscursive practices employed within her cultural environment: that is, by means of the way the inhabitants of that environment (caregivers, siblings, peers, etc.) talk about (and respond to talk about) the child's, their own, and others' communicational behavior. By learning how to participate in talk-about-talk, we learn how its characteristics matter to those we engage with and learn to make its characteristics matter to us in various ways. It is by this means that the child comes to acquire what, in the professional metadiscourse of linguistics, is called "linguistic knowledge." Moreover, meta-discursive practices vary significantly between cultures, as well as between smaller communities within a given lan-guaculture, although this is typically obscured by the cultural hegemony of literacy-imbued Western language ideology. Ac-cordingly, members of different cultural groups and sub-groups should not be expected all to construct in the same way what "language"—and "knowing language"—is for them. Theorists of language development need to recognize these cultural differences in metadiscursive practices and refrain from assuming that such practices—or the knowledge that they yield—are cultural universals.

The most immediate benefit of these recommendations would be to refocus language developmental research on the circumstantial contexts within which children develop their communicational skills. This methodological shift ought to be one which fits well with the theoretical perspective of integra-tionism. For those contexts within which the child learns to participate linguistically are fundamentally personal; but they are also fundamentally cultural and interactional. They are, in other words, fundamentally integrational. By refocusing atten-tion on the reflexive character of the child's experience of lan-guage, language developmental research would no longer seek to address a misleading and myth-based question about the ac-quisition of abstract items of linguistic knowledge. Nor, there-fore, in order to answer this question, would it be led to pro-pose the existence of cognitive structures or language faculties conceived as innate endowments of the human brain. Instead, the study of language development would shift its searchlight onto the real personal, social, and interactional contexts within which the child's developing communicational abilities are reflexively guided and shaped.

References

Peterson, C., 1990. The who, when, and where of early narratives. *Journal of Child Language* 17, 433–455.

Taylor, T.J., 1997. *Theorizing Language: Analysis, Normativity, Rhetoric, History*. Pergamon Press, Oxford.

Taylor, T.J., 2000. Language constructing language: the implications of reflexivity for linguistic theory. *Language Sciences* 22 (4), 483–499.

Taylor, T.J., 2010. Where does language come from? The role of reflexive enculturation in language development. *Language Sciences* 32 (1), 14–27.

Taylor, T.J., Shanker, S.G., 2003. Rethinking language acquisition: what children learn. In: Davis, H., Taylor, T.J. (Eds.), *Rethinking Linguistics*. Routledge, London, pp. 151–170.

Wittgenstein, L., 2009 [1953]. *Philosophical Investigations*. Wiley-Blackwell, Oxford.

IV

Understanding others and understanding language: how do children do it?

Abstract

Does the child's emerging understanding of other minds interact with his/her growing understanding of language? If so, in what ways? This paper focuses on the recent proposals of Daniel Hutto and colleagues regarding the role played by the child's developing skills in narrative discourse in his/her acquisition of folk-psychological understanding. What must the child understand about the properties and powers of language in order to become a competent participant in narrative exchanges and so, according to the proponents of Hutto's narrative-practice approach, acquire an understanding of other people's thoughts, beliefs, desires, intentions, and reasons for acting?

1. Language and folk-psychological understanding

> How we learn, as initiates into a practice, is constitutive of what we learn. (Williams, 2010, p. 21)

This paper addresses the growing interest in recent years—among philosophers of mind, cognitive scientists, and developmental psychologists—concerning the role language has to play in the formation—or, as some say, transformation—of the ordinary person's understanding of their fellow human beings' thoughts, beliefs, intentions, desires, and reasons for acting (Astington and Baird, 2005; Astington, 2006; de Villiers and de Villiers, 2000; Garfield et al., 2001; Lohmann and Tomasello, 2003; Milligain et al., 2007; Pyers, 2006; Enfield and Levinson, 2006). The study of our understanding of other minds goes under various labels in the literature, including "folk psychological understanding", "commonsense psychology", "theory of mind", "mindreading", "mentalizing", "social cognition", "metarepre-sentation", and "intersubjective understanding". While these technical expressions are not always synonymous, the differences between them—or between the members of the family of topics to which they are used to refer—will not be relevant to this paper's central focus or argument, and they will be used interchangeably.

More narrowly, the current paper focuses on the approach to this family of topics championed in recent years by the philosopher of mind Daniel Hutto and his colleagues, in particular on his proposal regarding the role played by the child's developing skills in narrative discourse in her acquisition of folk-psychological understanding (Hutto, 2007, 2008, 2009; Gallagher and Hutto, 2008).

Folk psychology is a philosopher's label for the practice of making sense of intentional actions, minimally by appeal to an agent's motivating beliefs and desires. It is the sort of thing one does, for example, when digesting Jane's explanation of her late arrival at a meeting because she mistakenly thought it was being held in a different room. Taking our friend at her word (i.e., if we assume that she had genuinely wanted to attend the meeting on time), we will blame the content of her beliefs for the confusion on this occasion. This is something we do, unthinkingly. We rely on it constantly. (Hutto, 2008, p. ix)

Folk psychology is . . . in essence, a distinctive kind of narrative practice. As such, it is a unique specialty of linguistically competent human beings. (. . .) The basis for this skill is sociocultural. (Hutto, 2008, p. 4).

In recent years, the dominant approach within the study of folk psychology has been what is called "Theory of Mind theory" (ToM) or simply "theory–theory" (Fodor, 1987, 1995; Gopnik and Wellman, 1992, 1994; Astington, 2006). ToM claims that a person's understanding of another's beliefs, intentions, desires, or reasons consists in a tacitly held theory: "a domain-specific, psychologically real structure, comprising an integrated set of mental state concepts employed to explain and predict people's actions and interactions, that is reorganized over time when faced with counterevidence to its predictions" (Astington, 2006, p. 180). Hutto and other proponents of what I will refer to as the "narrative-practice approach" reject the arguments of Theory of Mind theorists. In his *Folk Psychological Narratives*, Hutto argues at length that there is "no reason to think of folk psychology as any kind of theory at all" (Hutto, 2008, p. 10). Instead, as asserted in a paper he co-authored with Shaun Gallagher, "making explicit a person's narrative is the medium for understanding and evaluating reasons and making sense of actions" (Gallagher and Hutto, 2008, p. 28). Hutto and his colleagues argue that it is the child's growing competence in linguistic practices—specifically, in the practices of narrative discourse—which is the formative operator in the child's growing understanding of other minds. The child's ability to understand the intentions and behaviors of other persons is "not reducible . . . to the mindreading or mentalizing described by approaches to social cognition which presume a 'theory of mind'" (Hutto, 2008, p. 1). On the contrary, intersubjective understanding develops "along a route that . . . exploits narrative competency rather than the procedures, subpersonal or explicit, associated with traditional theory-of-mind accounts" (Gallagher and Hutto, 2008, p. 32). The most detailed exposition of and argument for this approach has been spelled out in what Hutto calls the "Narrative Practice Hypothesis" (NPH).

> Understanding folk psychology as a kind of narrative practice flies in the face of the prevalent view that reason explanations are merely a subspecies of theoretical explanations, the logic of which is structurally identical to the kind of explanations found in and throughout the natural sciences. (. . .) [E]veryday practical application of folk psychology should not be modeled on the way explanations are advanced in the purely theoretical, abstract sciences. (. . .) Folk psychology neither is nor can be suitably reduced to a tractable lawlike science. Understanding actions in terms of reasons is irremediably disanalogous to the way we understand the behavior of 'mindless' entities. (Hutto, 2008, p. 9–10)

The current paper begins with an exposition of the Narrative Practice Hypothesis, focusing on the role it attributes to language use in the formation of folk-psychological understanding. While this hypothesis offers an explanation of the development of folk-psychological understanding as a product of the child's engagement in narrative discourse, there is little discussion in the narrative-practice literature concerning the child's development of the linguistic understanding required to become a competent participant in narrative practices. For this reason, the major part of this paper will consist in a closer examination of the requisite nature of the child's linguistic understanding: i.e., of those properties of the child's understanding of language which enable her to participate in the very discursive practices which, according to the NPH, have a formative role in her acquisition of an understanding of other minds.

2. The Narrative Practice Hypothesis

In their paper, Gallagher and Hutto present the child's development of folk-psychological understanding as grounded in three intersubjective processes (Gallagher and Hutto, 2008). The first two of these—known as "primary intersubjectivity" and "secondary intersubjectivity"—have been the focus of the studies initiated by the pioneering research of Colwyn Trevarthen (cf. Trevarthen et al., 1979a; Trevarthen, 1979b, and Trevarthen and Hubley, 1978). Trevarthen and his colleagues claim that "the structures serving interpersonal communication are present in latent condition in the neonate" (Trevarthen et al., 1979a, p. 539). Their studies show that primary intersubjectivity is already detectable in the behavior of the newborn baby. Within only a short time after birth, babies distinguish between the things and the persons in their environment, and they perceive the actions of other persons as purposively directed. "In the second month after birth [children's] reactions to things and persons are so different that we must conclude that these two classes of object are distinct in the infant's awareness" (Trevarthen, 1979b, p. 322–323). Neonates imitate the faces of fellow human agents and engage in intersubjective mirroring and rhythmic integration with others (Trevarthen, 1979b, p. 333–334).

> [N]ewborns act in expressive ways that appear to be peculiarly human and highly sensitive to human presence. Most impressively, an alert newborn can draw a sympathetic adult into synchronized negotiations of arbitrary action, which can develop in coming weeks and months into a mastery of the rituals and symbols of a germinal culture, long before any words are learned. (. . .) Infants, it appears, are born with motives and emotions for actions that sustain human intersubjectivity. (Trevarthen, 2011, p. 121)

Between 9 and 14 months, the child begins to produce the behavior indicative of what Trevarthen calls "secondary intersubjectivity". At this stage the child becomes increasingly aware that the world of experience is shared with others (Trevarthen et al., 1979a, p. 561). She goes "beyond the person-to-person immediacy of primary intersubjectivity . . . entering into *contexts* of shared attention – shared situations" (Gallagher and Hutto, 2008, p. 23).

> Probably the most significant achievement. . . is the ability to be shown a new skill and to practice its potentialities under the guidance of another. This involves bringing an object freely into relations in a triadic person-person-object network—one in which each of the two persons shifts in awareness between the common object and the other. (Trevarthen et al., 1979a, p. 564)

It is during the child's development of tertiary inter-sub-jectivity that language is said to have its great impact. This is the time—which Gallagher and Hutto (2008) locate as from age 4 on—when the child develops a more mature psychological understanding of other people and their reasons for acting as they do. While children draw on their primary and secondary intersubjective abilities in the process of acquiring language, in turn, their growing competence with language lays the foundation for further advances in their intersubjective understanding. What the narrative-practice approach finds most important about the child's entry into language is that it enables the child to participate with increasing competence in narrative discourse and in related imaginative and pretend-play activities, initially supported by the "scaffolding" assistance of caregivers and other competent members within the child's developmental environment (Gallagher and Hutto, 2008, p. 28).

> For example in acts of storytelling such active support takes the form of children being prompted to answer certain questions and by having their attention directed at particular events. In the case of folk psychological narratives this will normally involve jointly attending to mentalistic terms such as "wish", "believe" and "know" and discussing what the story characters know, feel and want. During this process children learn how these states of mind behave in relation to each other and other terms in the psychological family. (. . .) This proposal is consistent with a number of recent empirical studies that have established that there are important links between narrative abilities and our capacity to understand others (Astington, 1990; Dunn, 1991; Feldman et al., 1990; Lewis, 1994; Lewis et al., 1994; Nelson, 2007; Peterson and McCabe, 1994). Exposure to stories is a critical determiner of folk-psychological

abilities and it has been shown that this relation is stronger than mere correlation. (Gallagher and Hutto, 2008, p. 28–29)

While the child's developing ability within the discursive practices of narrative guides her to a more mature understanding of other people and of the reasons why they act as they do, narrative competence is also claimed to assist her in acquiring—and, bit by bit, conforming to—cultural norms of behavior. By means of her growing familiarity with narrative accounts and explanations, the child learns how others should act, as well as how she should act herself. In other words, her increasingly sophisticated participation in narrative practices familiarizes the child with the normative expectations of interpersonal life in her community and with the possible consequences when someone does not meet those expectations.

[S]tories teach us . . . what we and others ought to do (and thus what 'we' are likely to do). And they teach us what 'we' ought to think and feel in particular circumstances. Stories therefore help to shape our common cultural expectations, making us familiar with the norms governing actions in 'ordinary' situations. They are an important source of guidance about the boundaries between what is acceptable and what is not. (Hutto, 2008, p. 37)

To summarize: from the perspective of the narrative-practice approach, the child's increasingly competent participation in narrative practices is a crucial ingredient in her development of folk-psychological understanding and in her maturation as a member of the sociocultural community.

What begins as perceptual and emotional resonance processes in early infancy, which allow us to pick up the feelings and intentions of others from their movements, gestures, and facial expressions, feeds into the development of a more nuanced understanding of how and why people act as they do, found in our ability to frame their actions, and our own, in narrative ways. Our everyday abilities for intersubjective engagement and interaction are, in the later stages of childhood, transformed by encounters with narratives. It is exposure to these complex objects of joint attention – and not facility with theoretical knowledge or simulative routines – that is responsible for the development of sophisticated folk psychological abilities and understanding; abilities which remain importantly in play in our adult life. (Gallagher and Hutto, 2008, p. 34–35)

While there are several intriguing questions stimulated by the narrative-practice approach—such as the cultural variability of narrative practices and its effect on the diversity of forms taken by folk-psychological understanding—my intention here is to focus on the following question. How does the child develop the linguistic understanding required to participate in those narrative practices which are fundamental to acquiring an understanding of other minds? In the burgeoning literature of the narrative-practice approach little is said on this subject. Yet in order to ground the NPH and its distinctive approach to folk psychological understanding, and to the child's sociocultural development more generally, it clearly merits more attention.

3. Metadiscursive understanding

What must someone understand about the properties of language and verbal experience in order to make sense of and participate competently in the discursive practices of narrative? As is well known, there is considerable disagreement about what linguistic knowledge consists in and therefore about what would be required to understand a simple narrative utterance – just as there is little agreement regarding the elements of folk-psychological understanding which are required to be a competent participant in sociocultural life. I do not intend to enter these theoretical quarrels here. My intention instead is simply to foreground what I assume are some relatively uncontentious properties of the competent speaker-hearer's understanding of discourse, in an attempt to open up a new avenue for approaching the question of how the child acquires them.

Imagine that my colleague John is told a version of a well-known story. He is hearing it for the first time. The narrator tells him that the story is about a little girl named Little Red Riding Hood. (This modified version of the traditional narrative is derived from Lillard, 1997, p. 268).

> *In the forest, Little Red Riding Hood meets a woodcutter, who says that her grandmother is sick. She understands what the woodcutter tells her. She wants to make her grandmother feel better, so she brings a basket of treats through the woods to her grandmother's house. When she arrives there, she sees the wolf in her grandmother's bed, but she falsely believes that the wolf is her grandmother. When she realizes it is a wolf, she is frightened and runs away, because she knows wolves can hurt people. The wolf, who indeed wants to eat her, leaps out of the bed and runs after her trying to catch her.*

Hutto (2008, p. 30) uses the story of Little Red Riding Hood to tease out the extent to which understanding reasons for acting is important in narrative. But it can also be used to bring into the foreground questions about the understanding of language and verbal experience which is crucial to one's ability to understand narrative discourse.

For the purposes of this discussion, we will presume that John understands the story as it is told to him. Given this premise, we would typically take it for granted that John understands that the narrator is talking about a little girl and about events in which she took part. He understands that the expressions "Little Red Riding Hood", "the little girl", "she", and "her" all refer to this same little girl whereas, for instance, "the woodcutter" refers to someone else. He understands that the phrase "the wolf" means a kind of dangerous animal and that the phrase "she falsely believes that the wolf is her grandmother" means that it is not true that the wolf is her grandmother. John also presumably knows that the girl understands what the woodcutter tells her at the beginning of the story, namely, that her grandmother is sick. In other words, John's comprehension of this narrative relies on some particular items of linguistic understanding. I will focus on the following selection:

1. He understands that the narrator is *talking about* a little girl and about what happened to her.
2. He understands that the expressions "Little Red Riding Hood", "she", and "her" *refer* to the same little girl and that the expression "the woodcutter" *refers* to another person in the story.
3. He understands that the phrase "the wolf" *means* a kind of dangerous animal and that the phrase "she is frightened" means that she is afraid.
4. He understands that the phrase "she falsely believes that the wolf is her grandmother" means that it is *not true* that the wolf is her grandmother.

5. He understands that the little girl *understands* what the
    wood cutter says to her, namely, that her grandmother
    is sick.

Again, it is not my intention to make contentious claims regarding different theories of linguistic understanding. I assume that 1–5 are propositions which commonsense would incline us to take for granted, given our acceptance of the premise that John understands the story. After all, what if it emerged in subsequent exchanges that, in fact, John does *not* understand that the narrator is talking about events involving a little girl, her grandmother, a woodcutter, and a wolf? Or that he does not understand that the expressions "Little Red Riding Hood", "she", and "her" all refer to the little girl? Or that the phrase "the wolf" means a kind of dangerous animal? Or that the little girl understands what the woodcutter says to her? If it turned out that John does not understand these things, would we not then be inclined to conclude that John doesn't really understand the story? And yet the premise we began with is that *John does understand the story*. It seems clear, therefore, that if we determined from his subsequent behavior that 1–5 are false—that he does *not* understand these things—then commonsense would lead us to conclude that, even though he was smiling and attentive as we recounted the story to him, *he does not in fact understand it*. Perhaps he wasn't listening. Or he couldn't hear us clearly. Or he has had a sudden brain seizure. Or he is blind drunk. Or we were mistaken in thinking that he speaks English. Or he is in fact a robot. Etc. All things being equal, having accepted the initial premise—John understands the story—we will naturally take it for granted that 1–5 are also true.

To get a closer look at the linguistic understanding we typically attribute to someone who understands a narrative, it is instructive to follow this reasoning a step further.

i. Can anyone understand that a particular stretch of discourse is about X if they do not know what it is for an utterance *to be about* something?

ii. Can anyone understand that a particular expression refers to X if they do not know what it is for an expression *to refer* to something?

iii. Can anyone understand that a particular expression means X if they do not know what it is for an expression *to mean* something?

iv. Can anyone understand that X is not true if they do not understand what it is *to be true* or *to be false*?

v. Can anyone understand that a person understands what is said to them if they do not know what it is *to understand* or *to say* something?

Quite obviously, each of the questions in i–v is intended as a rhetorical question. That is, to each the implied reply is "No, they cannot". If subsequent interaction with John revealed that he does not understand, e.g., what it is for a stretch of discourse to be about something, then we could hardly maintain that that he understands *that a particular utterance U is about such-and-such*. If John somehow shows that he does not understand what it is for an expression to refer to someone, then it can make little sense to say that he understands *that a particular expression E refers to so-and-so*. And so on. Apparently, then, the question concerning what is involved in John's understanding of the story is more complicated than it first seemed. For, given the premise that John understands the story—and hence the truth of 1–5 above—the

conclusion to which we are drawn by the rhetorical questions
i-v is the following list of metadiscursive propositions:

1'. John understands what it is for a stretch of discourse to be about something. (Intentionality)

2'. John understands what it is for an expression to refer to something. (Reference)

3'. John understands what it is for an expression to
mean something. (Meaning)

4'. John understands what it is for something to be
true or false. (Truth)

5'. John understands what it is to understand something said to you. (Understanding)

The reasoning traced in this section leads to the conclusion that the metadiscursive propositions in 1'–5' must be
true of John, for if any of them were false, then one or more of
1–5 would be false. Yet, as we have already seen, *given our
premise that John understands the story*, 1–5 must be true.
Therefore, 1'–5' must also be true of John. Another way of
putting this is in terms of what is presupposed by the possession of certain folk-metadiscursive *concepts*. (My choice here
of the adjective "metadiscursive" is not intended to be exclu-
sive of other possible terms: e.g., "metapragmatic" [Silver-
stein, 1983], "metacommunicative" [Taylor, 1992], "metalinguistic" [Love, 2004, 2007], or "reflexive" [Lucy, 1993; Taylor, 1997].) For example: if J does not understand what it is for
an expression E to refer to a referent R—that is, does not possess the concept of reference—then he does not (cannot) understand that a particular uttered occurrence of E (e.g., "she")

refers to a particular R (the little girl). This same reasoning would also apply, mutatis mutandis, to the other metadiscursive concepts noted in the parentheses in 1'–5' and to the metadiscursive propositions asserted of John in 1–5. Nevertheless, none of this should be taken to imply that John necessarily understands or has productive use of such semi-technical terms and turns of phrase as "refers to", "means that", or even "is true". Claiming that someone possesses the metadiscursive concepts and understanding which are attributed to John in 1'–5' does *not* amount to claiming that he has acquired any sophisticated metalinguistic or metadiscursive terms. Nevertheless, the reasoning followed in this section yields the conclusion that the conceptual understanding—which those technical terms are simply one, professionally-sanctioned way of expressing—must be in John's possession. For if subsequent interactions with John revealed that he does not understand these things, then it would be, to say the least, strange, even self-contradictory, to maintain that, all the same, he understands the expressions and utterances which make up the story.

So it seems that anyone who understands a simple narrative such as "Little Red Riding Hood" must possess a measure of folk-metadiscursive understanding. Thus, for the maturing child to progress from first and secondary intersubjectivity to the folk-psychological understanding which, according to the NPH, is the outcome of her increasing competence in narrative practices, the child must somehow have acquired this metadiscursive understanding. But how?

We are led, in other words, to a paradoxical dilemma. For it is difficult to see how a child could possibly acquire such general concepts of metadiscursive understanding as reference, intentionality, truth, meaning, and understanding if she is not yet able to understand what the particular utterances she encounters in everyday discourse are about, or that they mean or refer to such-and-such, or that they are true (or false), or that she or someone else does (or does not) understand them. However, the other horn of this dilemma is no less sharp. For, as the reasoning above makes clear, in order to be able to understand the utterances in a story like Little Red Riding Hood— that is, understand that they are about events involving a little girl, that their expressions mean and refer to things, and that they may be true or false, understood or not understood—one must grasp such concepts of metadiscursive understanding as are attributed to John in 1'–5' . In other words, a child who is able to understand the utterances in a story must already understand the fundamentals of discursive intentionality, reference, meaning, truth, and understanding. Yet how can a child possibly have acquired this metadiscursive understanding?

4. Metadiscursive nativism

The apparent intractability of this dilemma is a powerful force motivating modern forms of metadiscursive nativism. Concepts such as 'meaning', 'understanding', 'truth', and 'reference' are, as the metadiscursive nativist sees it, part of the human genetic inheritance. Thus Stephen Pinker (1994) represents children as innately equipped with metadiscursive concepts, which they are predisposed to apply to the vocal behavior produced in their developmental environment. Newborn children the world over are apparently already aware that the sounds their mothers produce are instances of language and that those sounds are therefore endowed with properties such as intentionality, meaning, referentiality, truth, and grammar. In his *Names for Things*, Macnamara (1982) claims that the child is innately predisposed to recognize the referential properties of language. A similar claim is made by Bruner in *Child's Talk* (1983), while Fodor and other cognitive representationalists assume that the child is innately endowed with an understanding of both the intentional and intensional character of language (Fodor 1987). The developmental psychologists

Shwe and Markman (1997) maintain that children have an innate concept of understanding what is meant by an utterance; and, among their list of universal semantic primes, the linguists Goddard (2006) and Wierzbicka (1996) include the meta-linguistic concepts 'word', 'true', and 'say' as "innate and indefinable human concepts which provide the bedrock of human cognition and communication" (Wierzbicka, 2001, p. 507). In other words, the metadiscursive nativist takes the dilemma presented above to be illusory. Children do not need somehow first to learn sophisticated metadiscursive concepts before they can begin making sense of the utterances and expressions they encounter in their communicational environment, for that metadiscursive understanding is already part of the child's biological endowment.

Nevertheless, like other forms of conceptual nativism, metadiscursive nativism does not go unchallenged in the academic sphere. Can it really be true that infants in their first months of life somehow know that their parents' and siblings' vocalizations are about events, objects, and situations, that those vocalizations mean and refer to things, and that they may be true or false? Can such preverbal infants already grasp that speakers intend to convey meanings by the sounds they produce and that those meanings may or may not be understood by those who hear them? What could possession of such meta-discursive understanding really amount to, *before* the children are able to produce or comprehend any actual utterances? There are, of course, many researchers in the fields of language acquisition and child development who maintain that it is all too easy to plump for nativist solutions to such questions and that scientists should refrain from explaining-away developmental dilemmas by the postulation of biologically endowed concepts and mechanisms. But what alternative is there? How can a child come to grasp that her father's vocalizing has a meaning, refers to some particular thing, and is true (or possibly false) *before she has somehow learned what these and other fundamental properties of human discourse are?*

5. False-belief and the folk-psychological dilemma

We may find it helpful, in addressing this issue, to recognize that an analogous issue lurks in the literature on the child's acquisition of folk psychology: that is, in the rhetorical foundations of theorizing about the child's developing understanding of other minds. It is to this issue, and to the response developed by the narrative-practice approach, that I now propose to turn.

Occupying a central rhetorical role in the last 30 years of theorizing about the child's development of folk-psychological understanding is the well-known "false belief task" (Wimmer and Perner, 1983). False-belief experiments have been designed, modified, and applied many times in recent decades, and in several different ways. I will refrain from going into the details here, as the experimental formats and results will already be familiar to most readers. In its most basic form, the subjects in the false-belief test are children who are shown a video—or in some experiments are simply told—about events involving a boy who has been given a piece of chocolate.

[The boy] puts the piece of chocolate in the cupboard, then goes outside to play. While he is outside, his mother finds the chocolate in the cupboard and moves it to the refrigerator. When he returns to the kitchen to eat his chocolate, the children are asked the test question: "Where will he first look for his chocolate?" Children with a mature understanding of belief report that the boy will first look in the cupboard, because they recognize that the boy did not observe the displacement of the chocolate and therefore he still believes that it is in the cupboard. However, children who are still struggling with the concept believe that everyone else, including the boy, shares their knowledge that the chocolate is now in the refrigerator. These children ignore that the boy had no perceptual access to the displacement of the chocolate, and they report that he will first look in the refrigerator. (Pyers, 2006, p. 209)

The mainstream folk-psychological literature standardly takes false-belief experiments to show that by a certain age—typically around their 4th birthday—normally-developing children are capable of understanding that others have beliefs and that their beliefs may be different from one's own. However, younger children—because they do not yet have a mature concept of belief—fail to understand that the boy in the experiment believes something different from what they believe. So these younger children assume that on the boy's return to the kitchen he will look in the refrigerator for the chocolate, because that is where the children saw it moved to in his absence – even though the boy was not aware of this. The younger children make this assumption, it is said, because they do not yet have a mature understanding of others as epistemic subjects: they are not yet capable of grasping that another person has beliefs, desires, intentions, and reasons-for-acting, and that these may diverge from their own.

For the theorist who accepts the standard conclusions drawn from the false-belief and related psychological experiments, the following paradoxical dilemma presents itself. On the one hand, it would seem that anyone who, in particular interpersonal contexts, is capable of understanding another's beliefs—or desires, intentions, reasons, etc.—must possess some fairly sophisticated psychological concepts. For example, it is natural to assume that, if John understands that a particular agent A believes X or has a reason for doing action Y—the kind of understanding that older children manifest in false-belief tasks—then John understands what it is to believe something or to act for a reason. After all, how could John understand, e.g., that A believes X if John does not understand what it is to believe something? Therefore when, from around four years old, a child is able to pass the false-belief test—manifesting her understanding of others' beliefs, desires, intentions, and reasons—she must already grasp the conceptual fundamentals of folk-psychological understanding. On the other hand, it is difficult to see how a young child could even begin to acquire such sophisticated folk-psychological concepts if, in interactions with caregivers and peers, she does not yet grasp that they believe, desire, or intend things or that they have reasons for what they do. Yet the first part of this dilemma implies that she must. How can this be possible?

As Hutto and others adopting the narrative-practice approach have pointed out, this folk-psychological dilemma is a powerful motivation for the nativism underlying many Theory of Mind accounts of folk-psychological understanding. Fodor's conclusion, for example, is that "intentional folk psychology is essentially an innate, modularized database" (Fodor, 1995, p. 284; cf. also Carruthers, 1998; Leslie, 1994; Baron-Cohen, 1995; Segal, 1996; Scholl and Leslie, 1999; Gopnik, 2003). However, the narrative-practice approach rejects the idea that "folk-psychological abilities are . . . a kind of biological inheritance" (Hutto, 2008, p. ix). As we have seen, the Narrative Practice Hypothesis proposes a very different explanation of how the child develops an understanding of other minds. The child's folk-psychological understanding is acquired, not by theorizing on the basis of innate psychological concepts or constructing such concepts by means of an innate theory-constructional module, but rather by means of her increasingly competent participation in everyday discursive events of narrative: that is, in talking with parents and others about what a story character thinks or believes, what they want, why they act as they do, how their actions relate to their desires and intentions, and so on. Accordingly, within the narrative-practice approach the folk-psychological dilemma raised in the preceding paragraph simply does not arise. The child learns that other people believe, desire, have intentions, and act for reasons as a part of her developing competence within the parent-scaffolded practices of narrative discourse. "The practice of supplying or constructing [folk-psychological narratives] just is that of explicating and explaining action in terms of reasons. Folk psychology is . . . a distinctive kind of narrative practice" (Hutto, 2008, p. xi). Therefore, once the child has become a competent participant in narrative exchanges and story-telling, it is no wonder that she is now able to pass false-belief tests. Moreover, it is perfectly understandable that she was unable to pass such tests before she became a competent participant in the discursive practices of narrative. "[I]t is notable that many false-belief tests are presented in the form of a narrative and could be interpreted as tests for a certain level of narrative competency" (Gallagher and Hutto, 2008, p. 25).

6. The Metadiscursive Practice Hypothesis

Let us now return to the topic raised at the end of Section 2 above: the need for the narrative-practice approach to explain how the child develops the linguistic understanding required to make sense of and engage competently in narrative discourse. The central proposal put forward in this paper is that the analogy between these two theoretical dilemmas concerning child development—the metadiscursive-understanding dilemma presented in Section 3 and the folk-psychological dilemma presented in Section 5—should lead us to explore the possibility of analogous ways of addressing them. Accordingly, the remainder of the paper will present an analogous hypothesis to Hutto's NPH, which I will call the Metadiscursive

Practice Hypothesis (MPH). As I have argued elsewhere, I believe this hypothesis to be crucial to the explanation of the child's developing understanding of language (see Taylor, 1997, 2003, 2010, 2011).

Bit by bit, as the child matures, she becomes skilled in her family and community's metadiscursive practices. The Metadiscursive Practice Hypothesis proposes that the child's increasingly competent participation in metadiscursive (or, more generally, metalinguistic) practices gradually transforms her initial abilities in verbal communication—including what sense she makes of linguistic phenomena and of her own discursive experience. The child's initiation into metadiscursive practices begins with her responding in increasingly appropriate ways to the metadiscursive remarks made by her parents and by others in her interactional environment. The following are some examples of the metadiscursive exchanges which occur in notes taken within the 3 months following my daughter's second birthday.[1]

- Child: Want play with toys
  Parent: What did you say?
  Child: Play with toys.

- Child (*Talking on toy cellphone*)
  Parent: Who are you talking to?
  Child: Susie

- Child: Dollie
  Parent: Which one do you want?
  Child: That! That one! (*Pointing at leftmost of three dolls*)
  Parent: (*Holds up doll*). You mean this one?
  Child: Yah!

---

[1] This issue is addressed in greater detail in Ch. VI.

- Parent: Who is that? (*Indicating a small doll*)
  Child: Margaret
  Parent: Oh, but that's your name!
  Child: Yah.
  Parent: She's called Margaret too?
  Child: Yah.

- Child (*Standing in front of DVD player*): Kitty-cat.
  Kitty-cat.
  Parent: You mean you want to see the kitty-cat movie?
  Child: Yah, yah.

- Child: (*Says something indecipherable.*)
  Parent: What did you say?
  Child: Want more milkie!
  Parent: Momma said that was enough.
  Child: No! More!

- Parent: (*Touching own ear.*) What's this?
  Child: Ear.
  Parent: And this?
  Child: Nose.
  Parent: And what's this called?
  Child: Cheek.

- Child: (*Upset. Standing at barrier to staircase.*)
  Parent: What's the matter?
  Child: (*Says something indecipherable.*)
  Parent: I don't understand. You want to go downstairs?
  Child: Yah. Yah.

- Child: Me see doggie.
  Parent: No! Really?
  Child: Yah. Two doggie.

Parent: Did you tell Momma?
Child: (*Turns excitedly to mother as she enters the room.*) See doggie!

- Child: What that? (*Looking at a picture of a mango.*)
  Parent: That's a mango.
  Child: Mando.
  Parent: That's right. Mango.

- Parent: Tell Cara you're sorry.
  Child: (*Looks at sister.*) Sorry.
  Parent: Good girl. That's better.

- Cartoon character on television, looking at camera (and hence at child): Say 'abre'!
  Child: Abre.

Recent research has drawn attention to the frequency of metadiscourse in the child's communicational environment. In his study of "talk-focused talk" in Norwegian and American family dinnertime conversations, Aukrust (2004) reports that, of the 16,000 utterances in his corpus, some 1800 involve the use of one or other of three types of metadiscursive remarks. "On average as much as every tenth utterance commented on talk in one way or another, which was a higher number than expected given the little research attention that spontaneous production of talk about talk has received" (Aukrust, 2004, p. 189). Other research by child developmentalists support this assessment (cf. Aukrust, 2001; Becker, 1994; Blum-Kulika and Snow, 2004; Demetras et al., 1986; Ely et al., 2001; Hickmann, 1985; Levy, 1999; Quasthoff, 1995; Stude, 2007; Wootton, 1997). It is clear that the child encounters much more metadiscourse than has previously been recognized. Through her preschool years the young child's communicational environment is saturated with metadiscursive feedback of various kinds, addressed both to her own verbal behavior and to the verbal behavior of co-present others. She hears metalinguistic labels, repair initiations, explicit corrections and modeling, recasts, reported speech, normative and evaluative assessments of what she or someone else has said, requests for restatement and clarification, metacommunicational directives, explanations of meaning and reference, and so on. It is also worth noting that in an extensive study of the British National Corpus—although the data is not primarily child-directed talk—Anderson and his colleagues found that metadiscursive remarks occur in 11% of the 138,017 transcribed utterances (Anderson et al., 2004).

Over time, the child's competent participation in metadiscursive exchanges gives those who interact with her a stronger sense that she understands what is going on in communicational interactions. Her responses, verbal and nonverbal, are increasingly in accord with those of someone who grasps that a given utterance is about her doll or that it is about what her sister is doing, that the word *mango* means that fruit in the bowl, that her father does not understand what she just said, that what he said about wanting to eat her ear is not true, and that she is called Margaret. Her parents and familiar others take the increasing appropriateness of her responses in metadiscursive exchanges as indicative of the child's maturing linguistic understanding. Accordingly, they act in ways which manifest their growing confidence in her understanding; and—more and more—she repays their confidence in how she responds in subsequent, 3rd- and 4th-turn contributions to their metadiscursive sequences. In other words, as the child's participation in metadiscourse increasingly conforms to cultural norms and expectations, those who interact with her treat her as someone who, as we say in Anglophone metalanguage, understands what it is to "mean" such and such, what it is for an utterance "to be about" an event or scene, what it is to "understand" what someone says, what it is for an utterance to be "true" (or "false"), and so on. To put this in the technical terms of academic discourse, we could say that they treat her as someone who grasps the concepts of communicational intentionality, meaning, reference, truth, and understanding.

Eventually, as the child becomes more and more skilled in her responses to others' metadiscursive remarks, she begins to produce some of her own. Initially, these may be the kind of remarks that are said to be "implicitly" metadiscursive, in that they do not include instances of what are technically classified as explicitly metalinguistic or metadiscursive expressions (cf. Lucy, 1993; Agha, 2007; Hubler and Bublitz, 2007.) For example, when she doesn't understand what her sister says to her, the child says "What?" Or when she doesn't know someone's name, she says "Who's that?" Or when she hasn't learned the word for something, she says "What's that?" However, bit by bit she begins to master the productive use of the folk-metadiscursive expressions characteristic of her family and linguistic community: expressions such as "is called", "means", "understands", "is about", "say", "talking", "is true", "tell", "ask", "is right/wrong" etc. What is most important in this development is not the appearance of these metalinguistic terms in her speech but her spontaneous and appropriate use of them within everyday metadiscursive practices. In other words, it is not the properties of the pieces with which she plays the game which matter, but how she makes use of them when playing the game.

The child gradually becomes skilled in her speech community's ways of verbally reflecting on discursive practices. The Metadiscursive Practice Hypothesis proposes that, as the child's metadiscursive abilities develop, her understanding of communicative events is transformed—as is her understanding of her own linguistic skills and experiences. In an Anglophone speech community, she learns that utterances are, as we say, "about" things and events, that they may or may not be "true" (and how to tell), that what someone "says" may or may not be "understood", and that particular expressions "mean" this or that. She learns that some verbal behavior is what we call "asking", while other behavior is "answering" or "telling" or "whining" or "not listening" or "yelling" or "being funny" or "being wrong", and so on. In other words, while the child becomes increasingly competent in using and responding to the use of the verbal tools in her community's metadiscursive practices, she comes to understand *what* she and others are doing when they engage in communicational activities. More technically, we could say that the child comes to "conceptualize" linguistic activity—along with her own experience of discourse—*as language*: that is, as consisting in words, meanings, acts of reference, saying and requesting, truth and falsity, understanding and misunderstanding. Another way of putting this is that, as a function of the child's developing metadiscursive competence, she learns to 'see' linguistic phenomena and discursive experience within the folk-metadiscursive framework of her cultural community; and so, bit by bit, she begins to behave accordingly. In brief, we could say, echoing Saussure's classic dictum: "The object is not given in advance of the viewpoint". It is by means of her developing competence in her linguistic community's metadiscursive practices that the child acquires the viewpoint from which the linguistic identity of the verbal phenomena she encounters is to be seen, understood, and reproduced.

In order to appreciate the transformative role played by the child's development of metadiscursive abilities, it may help to imagine a child who, for some reason, never learns to participate in metadiscursive practices. This imaginary child is not able to produce the sort of appropriate responses which my daughter produces in the metadiscursive exchanges reported above – that is, verbal or nonverbal responses to others' utterances such as "What did you say?", "Who are you talking to?", "Who is that?", "What are you talking about?", "What are you called?", "Do you understand?", "Say that again", "Which one do you mean?", "Really?", "Are you sure?", "Do you agree?", etc. This imaginary child *never* comes to produce culturally appropriate responses to these and other metadiscursive remarks and questions; nor does she ever produce any metadiscursive remarks herself. It would seem inevitable that, as this metadiscursively blind child matures into adolescence and adulthood, she would find it more and more difficult to navigate through her culture's communicational activities. We can easily envisage the kind of challenges she would encounter in institutional circumstances, say, in school, or in dealings with government, the police, or the legal and commercial systems: that is, if she is unable to participate in any metadiscursive practices at all. However, no less difficult would be her everyday dealings with friends, neighbors, family, and others. For, after all, what would language be like for such a child? What would she understand about language, its properties, and its uses? What sense would she make of her verbal experiences and behavior, about the verbal behavior of others, or about the communicative practices of her community? It seems inevitable that the life of such a metadiscursively blind child would not be fundamentally different from those famously described in the essays of the neuropsychologist Oliver Sacks.

Of course, in the normal course of events, children do gradually master the metadiscursive practices characteristic of their families and communities. However, as this thought-experiment suggests, the child does not begin contributing to verbal interactions with forms of behavior which are "already language"—as Searle (1995, p. 73) maintains—or which she understands *as language*: as words, as meanings, as acts of reference and understanding, as being "about" things and events, as being true or false, etc. On the contrary, the child's utterances do not emerge, full-blown, with the properties that meta-discursively competent speakers take those utterances to have; nor does she understand her own utterances or the utterances of others in terms of those properties. A child's name does not enter her verbal repertoire—either productively or recep-tively—as a name. Her "requests" do not begin with the prop-erties which our metadiscursive commonsense attributes to re-quests (see Taylor and Shanker, 2003). Nor does the meaning of a given word ("hat", "mine", "need") or of a true statement ("Dog there", "I no like that") begin for the child with the properties that metadiscursively competent speakers take word-meanings and true statements to have, and she does not yet have the ability to understand them in such metadiscur-sively competent terms. The philosopher Meredith Williams makes a related point:

> What is distinctive about the learning situation is that the learner does not have the necessary background competencies that make what she does naming (when the child calls out 'ball' in the presence of a ball) or counting or identifying a pain. That background struc-ture can only be provided by the social environment personified in the actions of [those who have already mastered the practice]. The significance of this is that the 'judgments' of the child and the judgments of the adult cannot have the same status or mean the same thing to the two agents. . . (Williams, 1999, p. 193)

The core proposal of the MPH is that a necessary com-ponent of these "background competencies" is the ability to participate in the metadiscursive practices of the child's soci-ocultural environment. It is her gradual development of this background competency that eventually transforms what she does, and her understanding of what others do, into words, names, meanings, acts of reference and judgment, true (and false) assertions,. . . that is to say, into language.

7. Understanding language and understanding others

To conclude, I will return to two of the issues raised above in order to see what light is shed on them by the Metadiscursive Practice Hypothesis. Section 3 identified the following paradoxical dilemma. In order to understand the utterances making up a simple narrative, a child apparently must already grasp the fundamentals of discursive intentionality, reference, meaning, truth, and understanding. Yet it is difficult to see how a child could possibly acquire such concepts of metadiscursive understanding before she is able to understand the utterances she encounters in everyday discourse (including narrative discourse): that is, understand what the utterances are about, what they mean or refer to, whether they are true (or false), and whether she or someone else understands what they mean. It is this paradox which serves as a rhetorical motivation for the metadiscursive nativism discussed in Section 4.

However, from the perspective of the MPH, this paradoxical dilemma disappears. For it is by means of her participation in everyday metadiscursive practices that the child comes to see that the utterances produced in her communicational environment—her own utterances as well as those produced by others—mean things, refer to and are about objects, people, events, and situations, are true or false, are or are not understood, etc. In other words, there is no need for biology— or theoretical fiat—to endow the child with innate metadiscursive concepts. Her increasingly competent performance in metadiscursive practices provides her with the required "background" metadiscursive framework: that is, with all she needs to develop, albeit gradually, her grasp of the distinctive properties and powers of language and thus to transform her understanding of—as well as her mastery in making use of—verbal phenomena.

Another, more metaphysically cautious way of putting this can be derived from the commonsense reasoning made explicit in Section 3. The more the child develops the ability to participate competently in metadiscursive practices, the more we are given the grounds for asserting of her the kinds of metadis-cursive claims asserted of John in 1–5: e.g., that he knows the story is about events involving a little girl, that he understands that the expressions "Little Red Riding Hood" and "she" both refer to that little girl, that he understands that the phrase "she falsely believes that the wolf is her grandmother" means that it is not true that the wolf is her grandmother, and so on. The child's growing mastery of her community's metadiscursive practices thus provides a justificatory criterion for attributing to her possession of the metadiscursive concepts attributed to John in 1'–5' and conversely reduces to nil the force of the nativist's argument that those concepts must be part of the child's biologically-endowed preparation for language.

> To understand what it is to 'have' a concept one must ask what kind of abilities someone would have to have in order to satisfy the criteria for practical mastery of said concept. (. . .) We can specify what a child's command of any particular concept comes to in terms of the mastery of certain abilities (Hutto, 2008, p. 131).

The Metadiscursive Practice Hypothesis also suggests a necessary part of any adequate explanation to the question raised in Section 2 above: namely, how does the child develop the kind of linguistic understanding required so that she can participate with increasing competence in narrative practices, the very practices by means of which, according to the narrative-practice approach, the child develops her understanding of other minds? The narrative-practice approach takes the child's participation in narrative discourse to be crucial to her development of folk-psychological understanding. The argument in this paper is that the child's increasingly competent participation in *metadiscursive* practices is crucial to her developing understanding of and competent participation in discursive practices generally, including narrative practices. That is, it is crucial to the child's developing understanding of language, as well as her understanding of other minds.

In his groundbreaking writings on folk psychology, Daniel Hutto argues—against the dominant trend in the philosophy of mind—that there is no good reason to think of folk psychological understanding as a theory or structured body of knowledge. Nor, I would argue, should we think of our understanding of language as consisting in any kind of theory or structured body of knowledge.

> In sum, it seems that in using mentalistic concepts appropriately, folk psychological practitioners exhibit mastery of a highly structured skill. But admitting this does not entail that the folk are, even "deeply tacitly", in possession of and deploying a structured body of knowledge. The fact that folk psychological understanding involves mastery of a structured practice does not imply that the relevant concepts are simple, having only one determinate use, ... that they denote inner mental entities with causal powers, that the principles in question 'exist' as a set of intellectually graspable regulative propositions, or that the kind of understanding in question implies the existence of a supportive mental mechanism that ultimately sponsors the capacity. (Hutto, 2009, p. 210)

In the spirit of analogy which animates and gives structure to the current paper, we could also say the following. In sum, it seems that in using and responding to others' use of metadiscursive concepts appropriately, language users exhibit mastery of a highly structured skill. But admitting this does not entail that language users are, even "deeply tacitly", in possession of and deploying a structured body of knowledge. The fact that metadiscursive understanding involves mastery of a structured practice does not imply that the relevant concepts are simple, having only one determinate use, that they denote inner mental entities with causal powers, that the principles in question 'exist' as a set of intellectually graspable regulative propositions, or that the kind of understanding in question implies the existence of a supportive mental mechanism that ultimately sponsors the capacity.

Of course, such a conclusion would go against many of the received ideas enshrined in the schools of thought that have dominated linguistic theory for the past century or more (cf. Love, 2004). On the other hand, it might also be taken to suggest a potentially fruitful approach by means of which developmental inquiry could break free of the dilemmas and paradoxes that have long afflicted the study of how children come to understand language.

Acknowledgements
A version of this paper was presented to the Institute of Cognitive Science at the Universität Osnabrük. I am grateful to the Institute and to my host Rudolph Müllan for this opportunity, and to the College of William and Mary for continuing research funding and support.

References
Agha, A., 2007. *Language and Social Relations*. Cambridge University Press, Cambridge UK.

Anderson, M., Fister, A., Lee, B., Tardia, L., Wang, D., 2004. On the types and frequency of meta-language in conversation: a preliminary report. In: *Proceedings of the 14th Annual Meeting of the Society for Text and Discourse*.

Astington, J.W., 1990. Narrative and the child's theory of mind. In: Britton, B., Pellegrini, A.D. (Eds.), *Narrative Thought and Narrative Language*. Erlbaum, Hillsdale, NJ.

Astington, J.W., 2006. The developmental interdependence of theory of mind and language. In: Enfield, N.J., Levinson, S.C. (Eds.), *Roots of Human Sociality: Culture, Cognition, and Interaction*. Berg, Oxford and New York.

Astington, J.W., Baird, J.W. (Eds.), 2005. *Why Language Matters for Theory of Mind*. Oxford University Press, Oxford.

Aukrust, V., 2001. Talk-focused talk in preschools – culturally formed socialization for talk? *First Language* 9, 285-97.

Aukrust, V., 2004. Talk about talk with young children: pragmatic socialization in two communities in Norway and the US. *Journal of Child Language* 31, 177–201.

Baron-Cohen, S., 1995. *Mind-Blindness: An Essay on Autism and Theory of Mind*. MIT Press, Cambridge.

Becker, J., 1994. Pragmatic socialization: parental input to pre-schoolers. *Discourse Processes* 17, 131–148.

Blum-Kulika, Snow, 2004. Introduction: the potential of peer talk. *Discourse Studies* 6, 291–306.

Bruner, J., 1983. *Child's Talk: Learning to Use Language*. Oxford University Press, Oxford.

Carruthers, P., 1998. Thinking in language? Evolution and a modularist possibility. In: Carruthers, P., Boucher, J. (Eds.), *Language and Thought: Interdisciplinary*

Themes. Cambridge University Press, Cambridge, UK.

Demetras, M., Post, K., Snow, C., 1986. Feedback to first language learners: the role of repetitions and clarification questions. *Journal of Child Language* 13, 275–292.

de Villiers, J.G., de Villiers, P.A., 2000. Linguistic determinism and the understanding of false beliefs. In: Mitchell, P., Riggs, K.J. (Eds.), *Children's Reasoning and the Mind*. Psychology Press, Hove, UK.

Dunn, J., 1991. Understanding others: evidence from naturalistic studies of children. In: Whiten, A. (Ed.), *Natural Theories of Mind*. Blackwell, Oxford.

Enfield, N., Levinson, S., 2006. Introduction: human sociality as a new interdisciplinary field. In: Enfield, N., Levinson, S. (Eds.), *Roots of Human Sociality: Culture, Cognition, and Interaction*. Berg, Oxford and New York.

Ely, R., Gleason, J., MacGibbon, A., Zaretsky, E., 2001. Attention to language: lessons learned at the dinner table. *Social Development* 10, 355–373.

Feldman, C., Bruner, J., Renderer, B., Spitzer, S., 1990. Narrative comprehension. In: Britton, B., Pellegrini, A.D. (Eds.), *Narrative Thought and Narrative Language*. Erlbaum, Hillsdale, NJ.

Fodor, J.A., 1987. *Psychosemantics*. MIT Press, Cambridge, MA.

Fodor, J.A., 1995. A theory of the child's theory of mind. *Cognition* 44, 283–296.

Gallagher, S., Hutto, D.D., 2008. Understanding others through primary interaction and narrative practice. In: Zlatev, J., Racine, T., Sinha, C., Itkonen, E. (Eds.), *The Shared Mind: Perspectives on Intersubjectivity*. John Benjamins, Amsterdam and Philadelphia.

Garfield, J.L., Peterson, C.C., Perry, T., 2001. Social cognition, language acquisition, and the development of the theory of mind. *Mind and Language* 16, 494–541.

Goddard, C., 2006. Ethnopragmatics: a new paradigm. In: Kristansen, G., Ruiz de Mendoza Ibáñez, F. (Eds.), *Applications of Cognitive Linguistics*. DeGruyter.

Gopnik, A., 2003. The theory theory as an alternative to the innateness hypothesis. In: Antony, L., Hornstein, N. (Eds.), *Chomsky and His Critics*. Blackwell, Oxford, UK

Gopnik, A., Wellman, H.M., 1992. Why the child's theory of mind really "is" a theory. *Mind and Language* 7, 145–71

Gopnik, A., Wellman, H.M., 1994. The theory theory. In: Hirschfeld, L., Gelman, S. (Eds.), *Mapping the Mind: Domain Specificity in Cognition and Culture*. Cambridge University Press, New York.

Hickmann, M., 1985. Metapragmatics in child language. In: Mertz, E., Parmentier, R. (Eds.), *Semiotic Mediation: Sociocultural and Psychological Perspectives*. Academic Press, New York.

Hubler, A., Bublitz, W., 2007. Introducing metapragmatics in use. In: Bublitz, W., Hubler, A. (Eds.), *Metapragmatics in Use*. John Benjamins, Amsterdam.

Hutto, D.D., 2007. Folk psychology without theory or simulation. In: Hutto, D., Ratcliffe, M. (Eds.), *Folk Psychology Re-Assessed*. Springer, Dordecht.

Hutto, D.D., 2008. *Folk Psychological Narratives: The Socio-cultural Basis of Understanding Reasons*. MIT Press, Cambridge, MA.

Hutto, D.D., 2009. Lessons from Wittgenstein: Elucidating Folk Psychology. *New Ideas in Psychology* 27, 197–212.

Leslie, A., 1994. ToM, ToB, and agency: core architecture and domain specificity. In: Herschfeld, L., Gelman, S. (Eds.), *Mapping the Mind: Domain Specificity in Cognition and Culture*. Cambridge University Press, Cambridge, UK.

Levy, Y., 1999. Early metalinguistic competence: speech monitoring and repair behavior. *Developmental Psychology* 35, 822–834.

Lewis, C., 1994. Episodes, events, and narratives in the child's understanding of mind. In: Lewis, C., Mitchell, P. (Eds.), *Children's Early Understanding of the Mind*. Erlbaum, Hillsdale, NJ.

Lewis, C., Freeman, N.H., Hagestadt, C., Douglas, H., 1994. Narrative access and production in preschooler's false belief reasoning. *Cognitive Development* 9, 397–424.

Lillard, X.X., 1997. Other folks' theories of mind and behavior. *Psychological Science* 8, 268–274.

Lohmann, H., Tomasello, M., 2003. The role of language in the development of false-belief understanding: a training study. *Child Development* 74, 130–144.

Love, N., 2004. Cognition and the language myth. *Language Sciences* 26, 525–554.

Love, N., 2007. Are languages digital codes? *Language Sciences* 29, 690–709.

Lucy, J., 1993. Reflexive language and the human disciplines. In: Lucy, J. (Ed.), *Reflexive Language: Reported Speech and Metapragmatics*. Cambridge University Press, Cambridge, UK.

Macnamara, J., 1982. *Names for Things*. MIT Press, Cambridge, MA.

Milligain, K., Astington, J.W., Dack, L.A., 2007. Language and theory of mind: meta-analysis of the relation between language ability and false-belief understanding. *Child Development* 78, 622–646.

Nelson, K., 2007. *Young Minds in Social Worlds*. Harvard University Press, Cambridge, MA.

Peterson, C., McCabe, A., 1994. A social interactionist account of developing decontextualised narrative skill. *Developmental Psychology* 30, 937–948.

Pinker, S., 1994. *The Language Instinct*. Morrow, New York.

Pyers, J.E., 2006. Constructing the social mind: language and false-belief understanding. In: Enfield, N.J., Levinson, S.C. (Eds.), *Roots of Human Sociality: Culture, Cognition, and Interaction*. Berg, Oxford and New York.

Quasthoff, U., 1995. The ontogenetic aspect of orality: toward the interactive constitution of linguistic development. In: Quasthoff, U. (Ed.), *Aspects of Oral Communication*. Mouton de Gruyter, Berlin.

Scholl, B., Leslie, A., 1999. Modularity, development, and "Theory of Mind". *Mind and Language* 14, 131–153.

Searle, J., 1995. *The Construction of Social Reality*. Free \ Press, New York.

Segal, G., 1996. The modularity of theory of mind. In: Carruthers, P., Smith, P. (Eds.), *Theories of Theories of Mind*. Cambridge University Press, Cambridge, UK.

Shwe, H.I., Markman, E.M., 1997. Young children's appreciation of the mental impact of their communicative signals. *Developmental Psychology* 33, 630–636.

Silverstein, M., 1983. Metapragmatic discourse and meta pragmatic function. In: Lucy, J. (Ed.), *Reflexive Language*. Cambridge University Press, Cambridge.

Stude, J., 2007. The acquisition of metapragmatic abilities in preschool children. In: Bublitz, W., Hubler, A. (Eds.), *Metapragmatics in Use*. John Benjamins, Amsterdam.

Taylor, T.J., 1992. *Mutual Misunderstanding: Scepticism and the Theorizing of Language and Interpretation.* Duke University Press, Durham, NH.

Taylor, T.J., 1997. *Theorizing Language: Analysis, Normativity, Rhetoric, History.* Pergamon Press, Oxford.

Taylor, T.J., 2003. Language constructing language. The Leverhulme Lectures, The University of Edinburgh. <http://wm.academia.edu/TalbotTaylor>.

Taylor, T.J., 2010. Where does language come from? The role of reflexive enculturation in language development. *Language Sciences* 32 (1), 14–27.

Taylor, T.J., 2011. Language development and the integrationist. *Language Sciences* 33 (4), 579–583.

Taylor, T.J., Shanker, S.G., 2003. Rethinking language acquisition: what children learn. In: Davies, H., Taylor, T.J. (Eds.), *Rethinking Linguistics.* Routledge, London.

Trevarthen, C., 1979a. Instincts for human understanding and for cultural cooperation: their development in infancy. In: von Cranach, M. et al. (Eds.), *Human Ethology: Claims and Limits of a New Discipline.* Cambridge University Press, Cambridge, UK.

Trevarthen, C., 1979b. Communication and cooperation in early infancy: a description of primary intersubjectivity. In: Bullowa, M. (Ed.), *Before Speech: The Beginnings of Interpersonal Communication.* Cambridge University Press, Cambridge, UK.

Trevarthen, C., 2011. What is it like to be a person who knows nothing? Defining the active intersubjective mind of a newborn human being. *Infant and Child Development* 20, 119–135.

Trevarthen, C., Hubley, P., 1978. Secondary intersubjectivity: confidence, confiding, and acts of meaning in the first year. In: Lock, A. (Ed.), *Action, Gesture, and*

Symbol: The Emergence of Language. Academic
 Press, London.
Wierzbicka, A., 1996. *Semantics: Primes and Universals*.
 Oxford University Press, Oxford.
Wierzbicka, A., 2001. Comments. *Current Anthropology* 42,
 506–507.
Williams, M., 1999. *Wittgenstein, Mind and Meaning:
 Towards a Social Conception of Mind*. Routledge,
 London and New York.
Williams, M., 2010. *Blind Obedience: The Structure and
 Content of Wittgenstein's Later Philosophy*.
 Routledge, London and New York.
Wimmer, H., Perner, J., 1983. Beliefs about beliefs: represen-
 tation and constraining function of wrong beliefs in
 young children's understanding of deception. *Cogni-
 tion* 13, 103–128.
Wootton, A., 1997. *Interaction and the Development of
 Mind*. Cambridge University Press, Cambridge.

V

Calibrating the child for language: Meredith Williams on a Wittgensteinian approach to language socialization

Abstract

This paper addresses the normative and reflexive foundations of language socialization. In several publications Meredith Williams makes a strong case for placing Wittgenstein's discussions of the normative character of social learning at the heart of an account of the child's development of language and mind. This paper examines Williams' argument, concluding that it needs to be complemented by an account of the child's scaffolded socialization into the community's metadiscursive practices. It is by means of the child's increasing metadiscursive competence that the child comes to measure the phenomena and experiences of language as 'we' do in 'our' community's linguistic-cultural world.

125

> When we abandon the reductive and other ambitions
> inspired by false pictures, and associated bad questions,
> we can see that the only legitimate question is how the
> child, and so ourselves as a species, gets into the
> normative dimension.   (Williams, 2010a, p. 199)

1. Introduction: The anti-intellectualist turn in the study of language development

Within the various fields of research focusing on child development, increasing attention has been given in recent years to the child's socialization within the normative practices of her cultural community. In this research, questions such as the following loom large: How does the child learn to form joint commitments and shared social goals? How does she become one who not only adheres to but eventually helps to maintain the norms and conventions of her culture's social practices? By what means does she come to understand—and, bit by bit, to conform her behavior to—the expectations, rights, conventions, rules, institutions, and obligations which constitute the normative foundations to social life and cultural understanding in her community?

Pioneering research on language socialization has been carried out by linguistic anthropologists, drawing on fieldwork in different languages and cultures. Using a largely ethnographic methodology, this research focuses on describing the widely varying cultural techniques by which the child is led to become an increasingly competent participator in the normative practices of her speech community (Schieffelin and Ochs, 1986; Clancy, 1986; Schieffelin, 1990; Ochs, 1996; Kulick, 1997; Brown, 2001; Kulick and Schieffelin, 2004; Gaskins, 2006; Howard, 2011; Duranti et al., 2011). Within developmental psychology, the work of Michael Tomasello and his colleagues stands out among many others (Tomasello et al., 2005, 2012; Herrmann et al., 2007; Tomasello, 2009; Gräfen-hain et al., 2009; Rakoczy et al., 2008; Rakoczy and To-masello, 2009; Rossano et al., 2011; Schmidt et al., 2011). Based on an experimental methodology, their research seeks to identify the specific aspects of the child's cognitive capacities which enable her to acquire social norms. In a ground-breaking paper, Michael Tomasello and his colleagues propose that

> ... the crucial difference between human cognition and that of other species is the ability to participate with others in collaborative activities with shared goals and intentions: shared intentionality. Participation in such activities requires not only especially powerful forms of intention reading and cultural learning, but also a unique motivation to share psychological states with others and unique forms of cognitive representation for doing so. The result of participating in these activities is species-unique forms of cultural cognition and evo-lution, enabling everything from the creation and use of linguistic symbols to the construction of social norms and individual beliefs to the establishment of so-cial institutions. (Tomasello et al., 2005, p. 675)

In what is a broadly interdisciplinary field of research, a third perspective on the foundations of the child's socio-cognitive and linguistic development emerges from the growing school of thought in the philosophy of mind which adopts a fundamentally anti-intellectualist and anti-representationalist perspective on cognition (Varela et al., 1991; De Jaegher and Di Paolo, 2007; Stewart et al., 2010; Hutto and Myin, 2013; Hutto, 2013). Of particular note is the "normative naturalism" propounded in the work of Meredith Williams. In her *Blind*

Obedience (2010a), *Wittgenstein, Mind and Meaning* (1999), and other important writings published over the past 25 years, Williams makes a strong case for placing Wittgenstein's discussions of the normative character of social learning at the heart of an account of the child's development of language and mind. Based on her readings of the later Wittgenstein's discussions of language-learning, normativity, and rule following—as these are found in the *Philosophical Investigations*, *On Certainty*, and the *Remarks on the Foundations of Mathematics*—Williams proposes an anti-intellectualist and anti-representationalist account of how the child comes to be a competent language-user and skillful participant in her culture's normative practices.

The second part of the paper consists of a synopsis of Williams' views on the normative foundations of the child's language socialization. The third part raises the possibility of complementing Williams' argument by giving greater attention to the role played—in both how and what the child learns—by the child's initiation into her community's meta-discursive practices: that is, into the community's commonplace practices of talking about (and responding to talk about) communicational activities. The paper's fourth and final sections consider Williams' notions of "bedrock judgments" and normative "calibration" and their applicability to our understanding of the reflexive aspect of the child's enculturation into language.

2. The normative foundations of language learning

To understand Williams' argument regarding how children learn their first language, we should begin by considering a foundational distinction made in her schematic picture of the language-learning process. This is the distinction between "the master" and "the novice" (also called "the initiate learner"). "The master–novice relation is the medium through which I…

construct (part of) Wittgenstein's views" (Williams, 2011, p. 199). Williams' uses "the novice" as a cover term to refer paradigmatically to the young child who is learning a skill, technique, or competence: e.g., the young child first acquiring a natural language (Williams, 2010a, p. 20). The novice is the child who does not yet have the basic skills or techniques to participate competently in the language practices of her learning environment: she is "semantically and epistemically innocent" (Williams, 2010a, p. 255). The "master" is Williams' contrasting term, used to stand for those who are linguistically-competent, skillful practitioners within those language practices.

> The terms "master" and "novice" are not to be found in Wittgenstein's writings though the expressions "child", "pupil", "instruction", "learning", and "mastery" are scattered throughout the later writings. I introduce these terms "novice" and "master" to keep track of certain important methodological and explanatory ideas to be found in the later work, especially in *Philosophical Investigations*, but also in *Remarks on the Foundation of Mathematics* and *On Certainty*. I use these terms to refer to the initiate learning relation between the child and the adult or the pupil and his teacher. These are situations in which the child or pupil does not have the cognitive competence required to exercise the skill that is the object of learning. There is an asymmetric dependence of the novice on the master, a dependence that is not epistemic but linguistic and causal. (Williams, 2011, p. 199)

> The value of the master–novice situation is that elements of language use "come apart" as it were, revealing the different dimensions of the background against

which we engage in our use of language. (Williams, 2010b, p. 355–356)

The diagnostic picture which Williams draws of language learning is one in which such novices acquire language by being brought up in the language-rich interactional scenes of the childhood environment: scenes which are normatively structured in a way that Williams' use of the terms "novice" and "master" is intended to foreground. Adopting the expression Wittgenstein uses in his discussion of the child's learning of names in the opening sections of the *Philosophical Investigations* (1953), Williams characterizes the process of the novice's initiation into verbal practices as "ostensive training". "Training is acculturation into a social practice" (Williams, 1999, p. 50). Within the normatively-structured learning environment, the child's initiation into verbal practices is "scaffolded"—that is, is supported or assisted—by her language-competent parents and other caregivers (the "masters"). This support helps the child to participate—in a limited way—within their joint communicational activities *before the child possesses the skills to do so autonomously*. Williams describes the asymmetric "scaffolding" (or "stage-setting") of the initiate learning environment in similar terms to those used by developmental psychologists such as Jerome Bruner, Michael Tomasello, Catherine Snow, and others (cf. Joseph et al., 2001). It is worth noting that these developmentalists have, like Williams, been strongly influenced by the later Wittgenstein's views on language and learning.

Williams affirms that, in order for the child to begin her initiation into her culture's verbal practices, the child must have certain behavioral and perceptual capacities as well as a common reaction to training. "Shared natural reactions, including ... perceptual sensitivities to certain physical saliences in the world and ... malleable behavior": these are necessary conditions for the child to become a participant within the culture's language-games (Williams, 2010a, p. 217). Without them, "training will fail".

> Training builds ... on the novice's innate repertoire of perceptual and behavioral sensitivities and her susceptibility to such training. As a matter of fact, we do respond with aversion to cliffs and loud noises and with attraction to smiling faces and red objects. We are responsive to sanctions, both positive and negative. This responsiveness is the novice's point of entry into the language-game. (Williams, 2010a, p. 105)

However, in contrast to many developmental psychologists and linguists working on language acquisition today, Williams adopts a relatively minimalist, anti-intellectualist view of these required capacities. Of greatest importance is her insistence that the cognitive and behavioral capacities which the child may be conceived to start with are necessarily less sophisticated than those that are to be acquired.

> The behavioral and perceptual capacities and abilities [required by the initiate learner] cannot be the distinctively linguistic competencies acquired in mastering a first language, without generating an explanatory regress. Initiate learning can only appeal to cognitive and behavioral capacities that are significantly less sophisticated than those acquired. (...) Ostensive training ... does not impute higher cognitive or epistemic competencies to the novice in order to explain lower-level forms of behavior. (Williams, 2010a, p. 105)

What Williams means by "sophisticated capacities" is clarified in various places in her publications. These include the capacity to form a hypothesis or interpretation, to ask for or understand an utterance as a name, to justify an assertion, to request, to report or describe something, to evaluate or affirm the truth or falsity of an utterance, and to doubt a claim.

> These are the sorts of things that a fully competent master of the language can engage in. They belong to the domain of the master of language. The domain of the novice, that is, the individual who has not acquired a language, who is an initiate learner, cannot make use of such devices as these, for they all already presuppose the very mastery that is the goal of the initiate learner. (Williams, 1999, p. 8)

Williams here reiterates an important point made by Wittgenstein in the *Philosophical Investigations*: if the initiate learner is represented as requiring some or all of these sophisticated capacities from the beginning of the language acquisition process, then the explanation of the child's ability to acquire language falls into a vicious regress. It cannot be that the child needs *more* sophisticated linguistic abilities in order to acquire *less* sophisticated linguistic abilities. For how, then, could we explain the means by which she is first able to acquire those *more* sophisticated linguistic abilities? Williams cites Wittgenstein's discussion of the way Augustine describes his initial learning of words: that is, by his parents pointing to objects and naming them.

> The conclusion that Wittgenstein draws is that naming cannot fix meaning, but is itself a semantically sophisticated act that presupposes a great deal of cognitive stage setting and language use: "only someone who already knows how to do something with it can significantly ask a name" (Wittgenstein, 1953, §31). (Williams, 1999, p. 191)

Wittgenstein makes this point again in his *On Certainty* (1969):

> §536 Naturally, the child who is just learning to speak has not yet got the concept *is called* at all.
> §537 Can one say of someone who hasn't this concept that he *knows* what such-and-such is called?
> §538 The child, I should like to say, learns to react in such-and-such a way; and in so reacting it doesn't so far know anything. Knowing only begins at a later level.

Indeed, the threat of this explanatory regress is a strong rhetorical motivation for the nativist arguments of linguistic rationalists such as Noam Chomsky, Stephen Pinker, and Jerry Fodor (cf. Taylor, 2010; Taylor and Shanker, 2003; Williams, 1999). Nativists argue that, because the sophisticated abilities required for the child to begin acquiring language cannot be conceived *already* to have been learned by the pre-linguistic child, it must therefore be that at least some of these abilities are innate and hence available to the child as she begins language acquisition. Williams responds to the nativist's argument, pointing out that it is no help in explaining how a child becomes someone who can mean, refer, name, judge truth or falsity, and talk about states of affairs to say that the child *already* is someone who mean, refer, name, judge truth or falsity, and talk about states of affairs – that is, "to explain the acquisition of linguistic mastery in terms of the prior possession of linguistic mastery".

> [I]n a sense, naming is the last linguistic act performed, not first in the development of linguistic ability. (...) Therefore, in order to avoid the regress, one must find a way to describe learning such that the cognitive and

behavioral capacities the learner starts with are significantly less sophisticated than those that are to be acquired. (Williams, 1999, p. 192)

Williams concludes that while the child does indeed require some supportive stage-setting to assist her initial steps in language learning, this support comes not from within the child herself but from her gradual initiation into the normative structuring of the childhood interactional environment, as characterized by Williams' schematic model of the asymmetric initiate-learning relation between "master" and "novice". This support, as Williams argues, is both "physically necessary" and "logically necessary".

> The structuring provided by the adult is a necessary support both logically and physically for the novice's linguistic actions. It is logically necessary for it provides the system of background beliefs, actions, and competencies, the complex pattern necessary for the token-utterance to have significance and so be an utterance. It is physically necessary for it provides the actual training and disciplining of the novice without which the novice simply would not, as a matter of fact, be able to continue. (Williams, 1999, p. 196)

This is a crucial point in Williams' account of language development. We need therefore to clarify what she means by the normative character of the language-learning situation and by the distinctive role which these practices play in the "stage-setting" within which the child becomes an increasingly competent participant in language practices.

> Norm-governed practices of any sort can be distinguished from causally explicable behaviors in terms of

four features. First, the use of linguistic items or signs is an indispensable part of the behavior of the practitioners and the coordination of their behavior. Second, the behavior is normative in that it is appropriate or not, correct or not. Third, in being normatively constrained, the behavior is evaluable and thus subject to sanctions. And lastly, such normatively constrained behavior is culturally heritable; it is not just acquired, it is learned. (Williams, 2010a, p. 52)

Within the language-learning situation, it is the adult, the master of the practice, who is the judge of what, in the initiate learner's behavior, counts as an instance of a particular linguistic act—such as asking for a name, answering a question, requesting something, or reporting a sensation—or of what counts as going on in the appropriate way: that is, acting in accord with a given rule or norm. It is the master who evaluates whether the novice's behavior is correct or incorrect (Williams, 1999, p. 204), for only the linguistically competent master has the requisite abilities and normative authority to make such linguistically sophisticated judgments.

How is the supportive stage-setting of the initiate learning environment *"physically* necessary"? Williams takes the language-games repeated within such scaffolded learning-settings to serve over time in "regularizing" the child's contributions to communicational activities: that is, in bringing her contributions to conform to the normative regularities and patterns manifest in the behavior of the competent masters of the practice. Along the lines of the joint attentional scenes studied by child developmentalists such as Bruner (1983) and others, Williams explains that training within the initiate learning situation is "effective in enabling the novice to realize her more basic desires by shaping her behavior to conform to, or perhaps better, mimic the activities licensed by the practice or custom"

(Williams, 1999, p. 194). In this way the asymmetric structure of the normative master–novice relation is a physically necessary component of the initiate learning environment.

How is the supportive stage-setting of the initiate learning environment *"logically* necessary"? It is only the adult, not the initiate learner who grasps the relevant norms of the practices in which the child is beginning to participate. Therefore the child cannot yet intend her behavior to conform to the norms or recognize her own or others' behavior as normatively guided. She does not yet have a grasp of the norms or rules governing the regular *patterns* to which, through training, she has come to adapt her behavior. So she cannot, in the strict sense, be *following* the norms of the practice. "What the initiate learner is being trained into are pattern-governed behaviors; in other words, behaviors that are performed because they conform, or contribute to, a complex social pattern *but not because the agent recognizes and follows a set of rules* that may provide an abstract description of the pattern" (Williams, 1999, p. 195, emphasis added).

To illustrate, we might imagine an 18-month-old child who, for example, says "nose" when I point at my nose and "ear" when I point at my ear. When asked "Who are you, little girl?" she says "Margaret". She says "My chair" when someone is sitting in her favorite chair. She says "Go potty" and "Get dressed" in what seem to be appropriate circumstances. When prompted with the utterance "one", she quickly responds "one, two, three, four, five". However, this 18-month-old child does not recognize "Margaret" as a name (for as yet she has no concept of a name). She does not understand her production of number words as counting. Nor does she produce—or recognize—her utterances "Go potty" or "Get dressed" as requests or assertions or as meaning what we adults take them to mean. For, as yet, the child has no concept of meaning or counting or of requesting or saying that something is the case. Because of her training in the supportive setting of the learning environment, she produces the regularities and patterns of normatively correct verbal behavior but without yet recognizing her behavior as guided by linguistic norms or producing it intentionally in order to conform to the norms.

It is in this light that we can make sense of Williams' claim that, in addition to providing the "physically necessary" support, the normative structuring of the learning environment also provides the "logically necessary" support for the child's initiation into language. In other words, the initiate learner child does not begin participating in verbal interactions with the linguistic understanding possessed by the teachers. In particular, the preverbal child does not yet know what a word or a name or a number is; she does not yet grasp what it is to say something about some object or event; nor does she yet understand what a request is, or what it is to count or to answer a question or tell someone she is in pain. She does not yet grasp what a rule or norm is or what it is to follow a particular rule or norm. Instead, as a consequence of the "regularizing" effect of the child's scaffolded training within the normative learning environment, the child imitates the patterns of what her parents do – their verbal behavior and their responses to verbal behavior. The child thus produces utterances that have the superficial appearance of names, numbers, assertions, requests, referring, rule-following, and so on; and she responds to others' utterances in ways that look like she understands their utterances in such linguistically sophisticated ways –even though she does not yet herself recognize the utterances as what we linguistically competent adults take them to be. She does not yet produce or understand them as instances of the types of linguistic phenomena we (e.g., English) speakers call "names", "reports", "requests", "numbers", "answers", "counting", following this or that rule, and so on. "What is distinctive ... about the learning situation is that the learner does not have the necessary background competencies that make what she does naming or counting or identifying a pain. That background structure can only be provided by the social environment personified in the actions of the teacher" (Williams, 1999, p. 193).

However, the adults in the learning environment—"the masters of the practice"—*do* have the normative linguistic understanding which the novice child, as yet, lacks. Given the child's emerging conformity to the behavioral regularities of the practice, her parents and other competent speakers increasingly *treat* her utterances as instances of these types of linguistic phenomena: that is, as names, reports, requests, numbers, assertions, following this or that rule, and so on. As Williams put it, the masters extend to the initiate learner "the courtesy" of treating the child's utterances as genuinely linguistic instances of "saying what THIS→ is called" or of "telling us what her name is" or of "counting" or "asking for something". In other words, within the master–novice relation of the learning situation, it is only from the perspective of the competent adult's understanding—and from the manifestation of that understanding in how adults treat the novice child's utterances— that any of the child's utterances *are linguistic utterances.* This is what Williams means in speaking of the "logically necessary" support provided by the initiate learning relation. *Without this, "there is no fact of the matter as to what the novice ... understands or even is doing"* (Williams, 1999, p. 203).

> In this way, the background structure and cognitive competence necessary for language use ... to occur at all is provided by those who have been acculturated into the practice, while the initiate learner's behavior is shaped and made intelligible by this background. The cognitive skills of the teacher provide the 'bootstrap' for the novice. (Williams, 1999, p. 204)

3. Metadiscursive novices

This part of the paper will focus more closely on one point in Williams' argument regarding the role that metadiscursive practices (or what Williams refers to as "second-order" practices) may or may not have in the child's acquisition of (what she calls) "primary" or "first-order" linguistic practices. As we have seen, a crucial claim in Williams' argument concerns the linguistic and cognitive dependence that the initiate learner has on the competent adult. The novice's utterances do not have an autonomous status as names, judgments, requests, reports, or acts of reference or rule-following. Nor does the child initially individuate others' utterances as instances of such linguistic phenomena. The novice's verbal behavior *is what it is* only, as Williams puts it, "by virtue of a courtesy" extended to the learner by the masters in the learning environment. Nevertheless, we know that, in the ordinary course of events, the learner does eventually develop the competence characteristic of a master of the practice. The linguistic identity of the learner's utterances does not remain forever dependent on the "courtesy" initially extended to her utterances by her teachers. The child eventually acquires, as Williams acknowledges, the full "linguistic ability to engage in these practices autonomously" (Williams, 2010a, p. 20–21). In other words, even if we grant the cogency of Williams' account of *initiate* learning, it remains incomplete as an account of how the child becomes herself a linguistic *master*.

To complement Williams' picture of language development, we need to consider how the child's acquisition of the skills necessary for participating in metadiscursive practices contributes to her linguistic development (cf. Taylor, 2010, 2012). It is by means of her increasingly competent participation in the metadiscursive practices of her community that the child comes to grasp, bit by bit, what the activities and experiences of language consist in. Moreover, as a consequence of this emerging grasp of *what* she and others are doing when engaging in communicational activities, the child becomes an increasingly skillful *practitioner* of language—or what Williams calls a "master" of the practice. While Williams nowhere discusses at any length the child's developing skills in metadiscursive practices, it is clear that she rejects the idea that the child's metadiscursive abilities play a role either in *how* the child develops linguistic competence or in constituting *what* the child learns in learning language. The initiate learner does not yet have the skills to engage in second-order practices. "First learning to participate in a game cannot require mastery of any metagame" (Williams, 2010a, p. 105).

It is at first difficult to reconcile this argument with observational and corpus studies which increasingly show that metadiscursive activity is a common feature of interactions in the child's learning environment (Anderson et al., 2004; Aukrust, 2001, 2004; Becker, 1994; Clark and Wong, 2002; Demetras et al., 1986; Ely et al., 2001; Levy, 1999; Quasthoff, 1995; Stude, 2007; Wootton, 1997). From early on, children observe and begin participating in exchanges in which metadiscursive remarks play an important part: in exchanges between other speakers and in exchanges in which metadiscursive remarks are addressed to the child herself. Moreover, as the child's skills develop, her caregivers increasingly treat *as significant* her responses—or non-responses—within such metadiscursive exchanges. Bit by bit, the child learns to participate—first in her responses to others' remarks and later by her own productive remarks—in exchanges with others concerning what a given utterance "is about", what a particular word or utterance "means", what a thing or person "is called", what she is or isn't "asking (for)", what she was "told" or what someone "said" or "didn't say", whether an utterance is "right" or "wrong", and so on.

To illustrate, I list below instances of my daughter Margaret's participation in metadiscursive exchanges, as recorded in observational notes. The first of these come from just after her 2nd birthday. The second group is from the four months following her 3rd birthday.

2.0–2.3 years

a.

    Child: Want play with toys.
    Parent: What did you say?
    Child: Play with toys.

b.

    Child: (*Talking on toy cellphone.*)
    Parent: Who are you talking to?
    Child: Susie.

c.

    Child: Dollie.
    Parent: Which one do you want?
    Child: That! That one! (*Pointing at leftmost of three dolls.*)
    Parent: (*Holds up doll.*) You mean this one?
    Child: Yah!

d.

    Parent: Who is that? (*Indicating a small doll.*)
    Child: Margaret.
    Parent: Oh, but that's your name!
    Child: Yah.
    Parent: She's called Margaret too?
    Child: Yah.

e.

    Child (*Standing in front of DVD player.*): Kitty-cat. Kitty-cat.
    Parent: You mean you want to see the kitty-cat movie?
    Child: Yah, yah.

f.

Child: (*Says something indecipherable.*)
Parent: What did you say?
Child: Want more milkie!
Parent: Momma said that was enough.
Child: No! More!

g.

Parent: (*Touching own ear.*) What's this?
Child: Ear.
Parent: And this?
Child: Nose.
Parent: And what's this called?
Child: Cheek.

h.

Child: (*Upset. Standing at barrier to staircase.*)
Parent: What's the matter?
Child: (*Says something indecipherable.*)
Parent: I don't understand. You want to go down-
stairs?
Child: Yah. Yah.

i.

Child: Me see doggie.
Parent: No! Really?
Child: Yah. Two doggie.
Parent: Did you tell Momma?
Child: (*Turns excitedly to mother as she enters the
room.*) See doggie!

j.

Child: What that? (*Looking at a picture of a mango.*)
Parent: That's a mango.
Child: Mando.
Parent: That's right. Mango.

k.

> Parent: Tell Cara you're sorry.
> Child: (*Looks at sister.*) Sorry.
> Parent: Good girl. That's better.

l.

> Cartoon character on television (*Looking at camera and hence at child.*): Say 'abre'!
> Child: Abre.

3.0–3.4 years

a.

> Child: (*Pointing at figure in storybook.*) What's he called?
> Parent: That's Eeyore.

b.

> Child: (*Sitting next to parent. Plays with tiny doll.*) Her name is Margaret.

c.

> (*Parent interrupts child while she is speaking. Asks why she is fidgeting.*)
> Child: I not talking about that!

d.

> (*Father says he will tell mother that he and child saw the rabbit on their walk.*)
> Child: I wanna tell Momma!
> Father: OK. You tell her then.
> (*On returning home, the child excitedly tells her mother about seeing a rabbit.*)

e.

> Child: (*Sitting on toilet.*) One, two, three, four, five, six.
> Parent: What are you doing?
> Child: I counting before the peepee come out.

f.

> Parent: (*With child, watching cartoon character on television.*) What's he doing?
> Child: He saying "I'm the map. I'm the map."

g.

> (*Father pretends not to understand what child says.*)
> Child: You not listening. That not what I said.
> Father: It's not? I'm sorry.

h.

> (*Father comments on something child says to mother.*)
> Child: (*Addressing father.*) I not speaking to you.
> Father: Oh, well, excuse me then.

i.

> (*Mother says it's still dark outside, but then they go downstairs and see the sun is up.*)
> Child: Mommy you was not right. I was right. It not dark outside.
> Mother: Oh, yes. You're right. It's light now, isn't it?
> Child: Yah.

j.

> (*Father says he is going to eat child's toes.*)
> Child: (*Addressing mother.*) Daddy being funny.
> Child: (*Addressing father.*) You teasing!
> Father: No, I'm really going to do it!

k.

> Mother: It's potty time.
> Child: Mommy, don't say it's potty time. I don't wanna call it potty time.

l.

> Father: (*Points at wildflower.*) What's that called?
> Child: I call that a [*indecipherable nonsense word*]. (*Laughs.*)
> Child: (*After pause.*) Maybe Mommy know what it's called.

Father: OK. We'll ask her.

m.

   Child: (*Sitting near open window. Birds singing.*
      Addresses father.) Guess what?
   Father: What?
   Child: Birdy say "Tweet tweet".
   Father: That's a catbird, I think.

n.

   Child: (*Sees a red sign and a green sign by footpath.*)
      Maybe it says stop and that sign says go.

What are we to make of these exchanges? Even in the first group of examples, when Margaret is just 2 years old, it is clear that she is becoming an increasingly competent contributor to metadiscursive exchanges. That is, she is participating—at first by her responses to metadiscursive remarks rather than by using any explicitly metalinguistic terms herself—in more regularized ways within exchanges concerning what she or others "said", who she is "talking to", which of several possible referents she "means" by something she says, what her "name" is, and so on. What these exchanges index are instances of distinct types of communicational acts (saying X, talking to someone, telling N something, confirming the truth of an utterance ["Really?"]), linguistic experiences (meaning X or Y, understanding someone), and verbal phenomena (what X is called, what N said, a name), as these are characterized within the normative metadiscourse of the Anglophone community in which she is being brought up. At the very least, we can say that her responses are in accord with (Williams might say "imitate" or "mimic": Williams, 1999, p. 194) the kinds of responses that competent adults would typically give to the metadiscursive remarks that precede them.

At the same time, Margaret's interlocutors behave in ways that treat her responses as manifesting her understanding (albeit limited) of what she and others are doing as instances of such verbal phenomena. To put this in the terms used by Williams in her schematic picture of the learning situation, the "masters" in the exchanges are extending to the "novice" the "courtesy" of according to her behavior the status of normatively appropriate responses to their previous metadiscursive remarks. Moreover, there are no indications in the notes that this defeasible "courtesy" has been misplaced or is in need of correction in subsequent turns.

The second group of examples, chosen from just after Margaret's 3rd birthday, shows that she is developing a growing mastery of the *productive* use of some metadiscursive expressions. She asks what someone "is called" and declares what she wants a particular activity to be "called". She says what a doll's "name" is. She speaks of "listening to" and "speaking to" someone, of "talking about" something, and she characterizes saying "one, two, three, four, five, six" as "counting". She speaks of what a sign "says" and describes an interlocutor's utterance as "teasing". And she speaks of "telling" someone something, of what someone says being "right" or "not right", and of what she or someone else "is saying" (i.e., in linguistic terms, using "say" as a quotative). It is apparent in the notes that her adult interlocutors' responses to the child's metadiscursive remarks treat her as understanding the metadiscursive remarks she has produced and as using the various metadiscursive expressions in accord with the norms of the Anglophone practices into which she is being initiated. And, again, this "courtesy" extended by the "masters" is not shown to be misplaced or in need of correction by the continuation of the exchanges.

This paper puts forward four primary hypotheses:

(1) The child's increasingly competent participation in such metadiscursive—or "second-order"—practices is

146

scaffolded in the same way as is her increasing competence in the primary—or "first-order"—discursive practices of the asymmetric learning situation.

(2) The child's more competent participation in meta-discursive practices is a crucial component in her developing grasp of what she and others are doing when engaging in communicational activities – including what verbal 'things' they are instancing (meanings, names, what someone said, etc.) and the properties of such 'things' (being right or wrong)—as well as of the kinds of experiences involved in these activities (understanding what someone said, meaning X rather than Y, talking/not talking about X, etc.). In other words, the child comes to act in ways that *treat* those activities, phenomena, and experiences as instances of the distinctive types of linguistic furniture which constitute her community's shared linguistic-cultural world: e.g., in Anglophone communities, their metadiscursively constructed world of names, reports, meanings, requests, descriptions, and words, as well as acts of reference, counting, meaning, telling, saying again, talking about, listening to, and so on.

(3) The child's developing metadiscursive competence assists her in becoming a more skillful participant in those "primary" or "first-order" communicational activities and in making more proficient and normatively appropriate use of their constitutive properties.

(4) The behavioral manifestation of the child's growing metadiscursive abilities also inclines those around her to *treat* the child as a more skillful language-user, indeed, as someone who uses and understands language as 'we' (in 'our' linguistic culture) do. In other

words, her developing metadiscursive abilities provide an additional, important strut in scaffolding the child's emergence as a fully autonomous speaker of the language: linguistically maturing from a "novice", dependent on the competence and "courtesies" of the "master", to an autonomous "master" in her own right, equal in normative-linguistic status to the rest of us.

To be clear, these hypotheses are not intended to suggest that the child's metadiscursive skills serve as the epistemic or cognitive foundation to the acquisition of initial verbal abilities – nor that the initial development of what Williams calls "primary-game" skills depends on the *prior* acquisition of metadiscursive skills. These are positions which Williams explicitly and correctly rejects several times in her writings. On the contrary, what is being proposed here is that *the child's ability to participate in metadiscursive practices develops concurrently with her development of the ability to participate in first-order, primary practices*. To the extent that they are analytically (or indeed cognitively) distinct developments at all— and, at least at the early stages there is no prima facie reason to think that they must be—the child's gradual development of first-order and second-order abilities is inter-woven and mutually supportive.

4. Acquiring a second linguistic nature

In several places in her writings, Williams draws on Wittgenstein's well-known remarks about measuring practices and the standard meter bar (Wittgenstein, 1953, §50). This occurs in the context of discussions of what Williams calls "bedrock judgments of sameness" or "bedrock judgments of the obvious". These are normative standards by which the properties of the world can be "measured" (Williams, 2010a, p. 217): that is, judgments whether THIS object, event, or act is the same as THAT, or whether continuing a sequence like THIS is the same as

148

has been done thus far. Examples of such bedrock (or "para-digmatic") judgments include "This is red", "The sky is blue", "2 + 2 = 4", "This is a hand", and "That's a book". Drawing an analogy to the calibration of a meter bar or yardstick, Williams argues that, as a crucial part of their upbringing in the master–novice learning situation, initiate learners are "calibrated" for such bedrock judgments of sameness. The result of this training is that they come to see such judgments as "a matter of course", as "obvious", and to follow them "blindly". The child's calibration for bedrock judgments of sameness is the foundation to the child's initiation into the normative character of cultural life.

> Human normativity is expressed through bedrock judgments of sameness. These judgments constitute normative standards by which properties of the world can be measured. Understanding how this is so requires an adjustment to our understanding of the relation between normativity and causation. This can be seen in applying the model of the standard meter stick to our bedrock judgments of the obvious. Two exemplars of bedrock judgments are "This is red" said of a fire engine and "5 follows 4" in the natural number sequence. They are the sorts of judgments very young children acquire. On analogy with the standard meter stick, these judgments of the obvious are calibrations that the young child undergoes no matter what. The child is "scored" for color, for number continuation, for objects over time. This "calibrating" is a causal process, but in being so calibrated the child comes to judge the world for color, for number, for objects. (Williams, 2010a, p. 217)

In these passages and elsewhere, Williams characterizes the child's socialization into language by analogy to the calibration of a measuring device such as a yardstick or the standard meter bar. When the stick has been appropriately calibrated according to the community's norms of measurement, it becomes an integral part of the normative practices within which we derive judgments of the length of objects: for example, judging this wooden plank, this plastic pipe, and that steel beam to be *the same length*. Analogously, when the child's communicational behavior has been "calibrated" within the initiate learning situation, the child comes to produce normative, bedrock judgments within our language-games concerning objects, events, experiences, and so on. That is, she calls THIS and THIS "red" but THAT "purple", calls THIS a "dog" and THAT a "wolf", and says that THIS event and THIS event are "getting dressed", while THAT event is "getting undressed", and so on.

> To come to play color games requires that the novice be calibrated with the basic colors. Seeing a blue sky or judging whether this color goes better with that requires being able to judge the world for color. This is analogous to our judging objects for length. (...) [W]e must measure the world in one way or another. That is what it is to be a creature whose first nature is to acquire a second nature. We cannot but acquire such norms. (Williams, 2010a, p. 218)

In her discussion of initiate calibration Williams draws on the places in *On Certainty* where Wittgenstein's discussion of certainty is linked to the role that normative exemplars and bedrock judgments play in the ways we learn to participate in language-games (Williams, 2010a, p. 254).

> Every language-game is based on words 'and objects' being recognized again. We learn with the same inexorability that this is a chair as that 2x2 = 4. (Wittgenstein, 1969, §455)

Part of learning is accepting such paradigmatic judgments as certain, thus constraining the range of acceptable moves within the language-game. These judgments set standards for judging. If one cannot believe and act on these judgments, one cannot learn what things are called or learn to calculate or do science or history. (...) The doxastic attitude of the novice persists in the life of the master, underwriting the master's system of beliefs. Certainty is shown in our doxastic convictions and attitudes. (...) This animal-like unavoidable believing bridges our first nature to our second nature... (Williams, 2010a, p. 255)

The hypotheses given in Part 3 above propose that, at the same time that the child is being enculturated into primary discursive practices—that is, as expressed in Williams' analogy, at the same time that the child is being calibrated for colors, social relationships, lengths, events, and so on—she is also being enculturated into the metadiscursive practices of her community. The child is being calibrated for paradigmatic judgments of *verbal* kinds of things, acts, properties and experiences, as well as *non-verbal* ones. Socialization into her community's metadiscursive practices "scores" the child so that she "sees"—not in this case a "blue" sky or "five" apples or the activity "getting dressed"—but a certain pattern of behavior as "answering a question" or as "teasing" and another pattern as "a request" or as "saying what your name is". She "measures" one response to her utterance as "understanding what she said" and another as "not understanding" and "sees" THIS behavior as an instance of "telling" someone something and THAT as being "wrong". To become a master of the language practices of her community, the novice must learn to see as "obvious" such bedrock metadiscursive judgments and thus to treat certain patterns of verbal behavior as normatively similar—e.g., both as instances of "talking about X"—just as she must treat as a matter of course the normative similarity of THIS visual stimulus and THAT visual stimulus: e.g., both as instances of "red". She must come to judge the *linguistic identity* of such patterns of behavior—her own as well as others'—in terms of the metadiscursive standards of judgment with which she has been calibrated in the learning environment. *In the initiate learning situation the child's verbal skills are calibrated so that she comes to measure the phenomena and experiences of language as 'we' do in 'our' community's linguistic-cultural world.* This acquisition of what we might term, in analogy to Williams' usage, "a second linguistic nature"—that is, *a reflexive-linguistic nature*—transforms what the properties of language and linguistic experience *are* for the child, just as her calibration for colors, objects, and events transforms what the properties of color, objects, and events *are* for the child. Significantly, as the examples listed in Part 3 above suggest, her acquisition of the community's techniques of "measuring" language practices occurs at the same time and in the same learning contexts as does her acquisition of the skills required to participate in the very practices thus "measured".

Nevertheless, as students of language development, we must be wary of treating the child who is developing such bedrock metadiscursive skills as a "little linguist", acquiring items of epistemic information regarding *the facts* (real or socially constructed) of which linguistic practices are constituted. On the contrary, we should heed what Williams calls the "epistemic innocence of the child" (Williams, 2010a, p. 256), and resist the temptation to view the child's acquisition of bedrock judgments of colors, objects, events, and verbal phenomena as the first hypotheses of a little (linguistic) scientist. "The initiate learning situation is not an epistemic context but one of calibration and norm-setting" (Williams, 2010a, p. 237).

What the child learns is not an ever-growing system of propositions (nodes in a web of belief) but a complexity of behavior in which the use of words is an integral part (...). [T]he child becomes a participant in our various language-games. In doing so, she thereby judges with us that this is a chair and this is a hand and this is a zebra. The affinity with the primitive game of the builders is clear, and so are some of the implications. In this context, the most important affinity is that neither the builder nor the child, in their 'judgments', are entertaining existence hypotheses concerning slabs or chairs. They work with no hypotheses at all. Their believing is not of an epistemic sort and so cannot be modeled as a set of hypotheses... (Williams, 2010a, p. 256)

5. Conclusion: Language lessons for the masters

As institutionally trained theorists of language and language development, we must therefore resist the powerful temptation to theorize the initiate learner's metadiscursive remarks—or her responses to others' uses of such remarks—as standing in an epistemic relation to primary discursive phenomena. The child's doxastic conviction that *Margaret* is her "name" and that she is "talking about" THIS one and not THAT other one, etc., must not be construed as a junior version of propositional attitudes, indicative of dawning knowledge or belief. The sophisticated language-game in which epistemic statements about verbal phenomena are at home is not one which the child has yet learned how to play.

[Judgments of category membership] are part of the calibration of the participant within a language-game. Judging "that's a red cube" in the presence of a red cube is not a matter of "red" denoting a color patch and "cube" denoting a shape. Rather the sentence "that's a red cube" is *an alignment of the subject to a state of affairs in a way that the meter bar in alignment with an object marks the length "one meter"*. "Red cube" is a line of measurement on the human "bar". Individual marks are fixed by means of training into a social practice. (Williams, 2010a, p. 104, emphasis added)

Analogously, "talking about X", "asking for", "understanding", "my name", "wrong", etc., are lines of measurement on 'our' linguistic-culture's metadiscursive "bar". And judging "Margaret is my name" is not a matter of "Margaret" denoting a person and "name" denoting a linguistic category, but rather "an alignment of the subject to a state of affairs in a way that the meter bar in alignment with an object marks the length 'one meter'." Accordingly, we should be wary of the potentially misleading nature of the theoretical terms "first order" and "second order", as these are applied in researching the child's growing competence in metadiscursive practices or in characterizing the transformative effect that this growing reflexive competence has on her communicational skills more generally. In studying her developing metadiscursive abilities, we must resist treating the novice's initial contributions to metadiscursive practices as the making of the first, primitive moves in an epistemological (meta)language-game: that sophisticated language-game within which—and with the overlay of years of institutionalized grammatical education and normative-disciplinary training—we (supreme) 'masters' of language hold our own metadiscursive propositions accountable (Taylor, 1992, 1997). Such a decontextualizing of the child's initial contributions to her community's metadiscursive practices—compounded by their recontextualization within the epistemological language-game of the disciplinary metadiscourses of the language sciences—leads inexorably to the kind of explanatory regress that Williams and Wittgenstein warn us of.

While, as Williams argues, metadiscourse does not provide the cognitive or epistemic foundation on which the child's development of her primary linguistic abilities depends, the child's increasing ability to participate in meta-discursive practices does play a crucial role in how the child acquires language's reflexive character, *that which is distinctively linguistic* about culturally-mediated communicational behavior and experience: namely, its consisting of (as we say in the Anglophone cultural world) meanings, requests, names, questions, reports, repetitions of the same word, referring, saying it again, talking about, counting, being right or wrong, and so on. As the child becomes increasingly competent in her cultural community's metadiscursive practices, she gradually develops the full "linguistic ability to engage in these practices autonomously" (Williams, 2010a, p. 20–21). And, we come to see her and treat her as a competent participant in our language practices. As indeed she is.

This paper's conclusion is derived from reflection on the work of the philosophers Williams and Wittgenstein on the one hand and on that of developmental psychologists such as Bruner, Vygotsky, and Tomasello on the other. At the same time, it implies an important corollary for linguists studying language acquisition and language typology. *The reflexive-linguistic competence which the child develops by means of her scaffolded socialization into the metadiscursive practices of her community is far from being a cultural or linguistic universal.* On the contrary. On the one hand, there is abundant and ever-growing research by linguistic anthropologists revealing the widely divergent features and patterns of the commonplace metadiscursive practices found in different cultural communities around the world (e.g., Briggs, 1998; Duranti, 1988; Danziger and Rumsey, 2013; Hanks, 1996; Rosaldo, 1982; Irvine and Gal, 2000; Rumsey, 1990; Silverstein, 1985; Lucy, 1993; Gaskins, 2006; Nevins, 2004). What being competent is—what the criteria of autonomous "mastery" are—in a given language therefore varies according to the normatively-maintained, "folk" metadiscursive practices of its speech community, as do the properties and practices which are conceived to fall within the master's competency: i.e., the properties and practices which constitute her community's shared and familiar linguistic-cultural world. On the other hand, there are also many ethnographic studies demonstrating the cultural diversity of the language socialization practices of different speech communities (e.g., Ochs and Schieffelin, 2011; Ochs, 1996; Schieffelin, 1990; Howard, 2011; Clancy, 1986; Kulick, 1997; Kulick and Schieffelin, 2004; Brown, 2001; Duranti et al., 2011; Hickmann, 1985). In the context of such research, this paper's conclusion can be seen to yield another source of evidence and argument supporting the growing claims within linguistic theory that it is not universality, but diversity that is the hallmark of human linguistic ability. As the linguists Nicholas Evans and Stephen Levinson argue in their influential 2009 article in *Behavioral and Brain Sciences*, descriptive linguistic research of the past decades has revealed, contrary to the hypotheses of Universal Grammar, "just how few and unprofound the universal characteristics of language are, once we honestly confront the diversity offered to us by the world's 6,000 to 8,000 languages" (Evans and Levinson, 2009, p. 429). If this paper's conclusion is correct, then the child's initiation into her developmental community's metadiscursive practices is a powerful generator of linguistic diversity and communicational relativity – as well as being an important vehicle of linguistic-cultural inheritance across succeeding generations. It is, moreover, a process which, as Meredith Williams persuasively argues, we can only come to understand by devoting more research attention to the normative character of the learning environment and of the cultural practices within which the child's language socialization occurs.

Acknowledgements

Versions of this paper were presented at Uppsala University and at a conference held at St. John's College (Oxford) in memory of my dear friend Gordon Baker. I am grateful to these two host institutions, as well as to the College of William and Mary. Personal thanks go to Pär Segerdahl, Katherine Morris, Marie McGinn, Ann and Margaret Taylor.

References

Anderson, M., Fister, A., Lee, B., Tardia, L., Wang, D., 2004. On the types and frequency of meta-language in conversation: a preliminary report. In: *Proceedings of the 14th Annual Meeting of the Society for Text and Discourse*.

Aukrust, V., 2001. Talk-focused talk in preschools – culturally formed socialization for talk? *First Language* 9, 285–297.

Aukrust, V., 2004. Talk about talk with young children: pragmatic socialization in two communities in Norway and the US. *Journal of Child Language* 31, 177–201.

Becker, J., 1994. Pragmatic socialization: parental input to preschoolers. *Discourse Processes* 17, 131–148.

Briggs, C., 1998. "You're a liar – you're just like a woman!": constructing dominant ideologies of language in Warao men's gossip. In: Schieffelin, B., Woolard, K., Kroskrity, P. (Eds.), *Language Ideologies: Practice and Theory*. Oxford University Press, Oxford.

Brown, P.M., 2001. Learning to talk about motion up and down in Tzeltal. In: Bowerman, M., Levinson, S. (Eds.), *Language Acquisition and Conceptual*

Development. Cambridge University Press, Cambridge, pp. 512–543.

Bruner, J., 1983. *Child's Talk: Learning to Use Language*. Oxford University Press, Oxford.

Clancy, P., 1986. The acquisition of communicative style in Japanese. In: Schieffelin, B., Ochs, E. (Eds.), *Language Socialization Across Cultures*. Cambridge University Press, Cambridge, pp. 213–250.

Clark, E., Wong, A., 2002. Pragmatic directions about language use: offers of words and relations. *Language in Society* 31, 181–212.

Danziger, E., Rumsey, A. (Eds.), 2013. Intersubjectivity Across languages and cultures. *Language & Communication* 33 (3) (special issue).

De Jaegher, H., Di Paolo, E., 2007. Participatory sense-making. *Phenomenology and the Cognitive Sciences* 6 (4), 485–507.

Demetras, M., Post, K., Snow, C., 1986. Feedback to first language learners: the role of repetitions and clarification questions. *Journal of Child Language* 13, 275–292.

Duranti, A., 1988. Intentions, language, and social action in a Samoan context. *Journal of Pragmatics* 12, 13–33.

Duranti, A., Ochs, E., Schieffelin, B. (Eds.), 2011. *The Handbook of Language Socialization*. Blackwell, Oxford.

Ely, R., Gleason, J., MacGibbon, A., Zaretsky, E., 2001. Attention to language: lessons learned at the dinner table. *Social Development* 10, 355–373.

Evans, N., Levinson, S., 2009. The myth of language universals. *Behavioral and Brain Sciences* 32, 429–492.

Gaskins, S., 2006. Cultural perspectives on infant-caregiver interaction. In: Enfield, N., Levinson, S. (Eds.), *Roots of Human Sociality*. Berg, Oxford, New York, pp. 279–298.

Gräfenhain, M., Behne, T., Carpenter, M., Tomasello, M., 2009. Young children's understanding of joint commitments. *Developmental Psychology* 45, 1430–1443.

Hanks, W., 1996. *Language and Communicative Practices*. Westview, Boulder, CO.

Herrmann, E., Call, J., Lloreda, M., Hare, B., Tomasello, M., 2007. Humans have evolved specialized skills of social cognition: the cultural intelligence hypothesis. *Science* 317, 1360–1366.

Hickmann, M., 1985. Metapragmatics in child language. In: Mertz, E., Parmentier, R. (Eds.), *Semiotic Mediation: Sociocultural and Psychological Perspectives*. Academic Press, New York.

Howard, K., 2011. Language socialization and hierarchy. In: Duranti, A. et al. (Eds.), *The Handbook of Language Socialization*. Blackwell, Oxford.

Hutto, D., 2013. Enactivism, from a Wittgensteinian point of view. *American Philosophical Quarterly* 50 (3), 281–302.

Hutto, D., Myin, E., 2013. *Radicalizing Enactivism. Basic Minds without Content*. MIT Press, Cambridge MA.

Irvine, J., Gal, S., 2000. Language ideology and linguistic differentiation. In: Kroskrity, P. (Ed.), *Regimes of Language*. SAR Press, Santa Fe., pp. 35–83.

Joseph, J., Love, N., Taylor, T.J., 2001. *Landmarks in Linguistic Thought: The Twentieth Century*, vol. 2. Routledge, London and New York.

Kulick, D., 1997. *Language Shift and Cultural Reproduction: Socialization, Self and Syncretism in a Papua New Guinea Village*. Cambridge University Press, Cambridge.

Kulick, D., Schieffelin, B., 2004. Language socialization. In: Duranti, A. (Ed.), *A Companion to Linguistic Anthropology*. Blackwell, Oxford, pp. 349–368.

Levy, Y., 1999. Early metalinguistic competence: speech monitoring and repair behavior. *Developmental Psychology* 35, 822–834.

Lucy, J., 1993. Metapragmatic presentationals: reporting speech with quotatives in Yucatec Maya. In: Lucy, J. (Ed.), *Reflexive Language*. Cambridge University Press, Cambridge.

Nevins, E., 2004. Learning to listen: confronting two meanings of language loss in the contemporary White Mountain Apache speech community. *Journal of Linguistic Anthropology* 14 (2), 269–288.

Ochs, E., 1996. Linguistic resources for socializing humanity. In: Gumperz, J., Levinson, S. (Eds.), *Rethinking Linguistic Relativity*. Cambridge University Press, Cambridge, pp. 407–437.

Ochs, E., Schieffelin, B., 2011. The theory of language socialization. In: Duranti, A. et al. (Eds.), *The Handbook of Language Socialization*. Blackwell, Oxford.

Quasthoff, U., 1995. The ontogenetic aspect of orality: toward the interactive constitution of linguistic development. In: Quasthoff, U. (Ed.), *Aspects of Oral Communication*. Mouton de Gruyter, Berlin.

Rakoczy, H., Tomasello, M., 2009. Done wrong or said wrong? Young children distinguish the directions-of-fit of different speech acts normatively. *Cognition* 113, 205–212.

Rakoczy, H., Warneken, F., Tomasello, M., 2008. The sources of normativity: young children's awareness of the normative structure of games. *Developmental Psychology* 44, 875–881.

Rosaldo, M., 1982. The things we do with words: Ilongot speech acts and speech act theory in philosophy. *Language in Society* 11, 203–237.

Rossano, F., Rakoczy, H., Tomasello, M., 2011. Young children's understanding of violations of property rights. *Cognition* 121, 219–227.

Rumsey, A., 1990. Word meaning and linguistic ideology. *American Anthropologist* 92 (2), 346–361.

Schieffelin, B., 1990. *The Give and Take of Everyday Life: Language Socialization of Kaluli Children*. Cambridge University Press, Cambridge.

Schieffelin, B., Ochs, E. (Eds.), 1986. *Language Socialization Across Cultures.* Cambridge University Press, Cambridge.

Schmidt, M.F.H., Rakoczy, H., Tomasello, M., 2011. Young children attribute normativity to novel actions without pedagogy or normative language. *Developmental Science* 14, 530–539.

Silverstein, M., 1985. The culture of language in Chinookan narrative texts: or, On saying that . . . in Chinook. In: Nichols, J., Woodbury, A. (Eds.), *Grammar Inside and Outside the Clause*. Cambridge University Press, Cambridge.

Stewart, J., Gapenne, O., Di Paolo, E. (Eds.), 2010. *Enaction: Towards a New Paradigm for Cognitive Science*. MIT Press, Cambridge.

Stude, J., 2007. The acquisition of metapragmatic abilities in preschool children. In: Bublitz, W., Hubler, A. (Eds.), *Metapragmatics in Use*. J. Benjamins, Amsterdam.

Taylor, T.J., 1992. *Mutual Misunderstanding: Scepticism and the Theorizing of Language and Interpretation*. Duke University Press, Durham, NH.

Taylor, T.J., 1997. *Theorizing Language: Analysis, Normativity, Rhetoric, History*. Pergamon Press, Oxford.

Taylor, T.J., 2010. Where does language come from? The role of reflexive enculturation in language development. *Language Sciences* 32 (1), 14–27.

Taylor, T.J., 2012. Understanding others and understanding language: how do children do it? *Language Sciences* 34 (1), 1–12.

Taylor, T.J., Shanker, T.J., 2003. Rethinking language acquisition: what children learn. In: Davies, H., Taylor, T.J. (Eds.), *Rethinking Linguistics*. Routledge, London.

Tomasello, M., 2009. *Why We Cooperate*. MIT Press, Cambridge, MA.

Tomasello, M., Carpenter, M., Call, J., Behne, T., Moll, H., 2005. Understanding and sharing intentions: the origins of cultural cognition. *Behavioral and Brain Sciences* 28, 675–691.

Tomasello, M., Melis, A.P., Tennie, C., Wyman, E., Herrmann, E., 2012. Two key steps in the evolution of human cooperation: the interdependence hypothesis. *Current Anthropology* 53 (6).

Varela, F., Thompson, E., Rosch, E., 1991. *The Embodied Mind: Cognitive Science and Human Experience*. MIT Press, Cambridge.

Williams, M., 1999. *Wittgenstein, Mind and Meaning: Towards a Social Conception of Mind*. Routledge, London and New York.

Williams, M., 2010a. *Blind Obedience: The Structure and Content of Wittgenstein's Later Philosophy*. Routledge, London and New York.

Williams, M., 2010b. Normative naturalism. *International Journal of Philosophical Studies* 18 (3), 355–375.

Williams, M., 2011. Master and novice in the later Wittgenstein. In: Moyal-Sharrock, D. (Ed.). *American Philosophical Quarterly* 48 (2), 199–211.

Wittgenstein, L., 1953. *Philosophical Investigations*. Blackwell, Oxford.

Wittgenstein, L., 1969. *On Certainty*. Blackwell, Oxford.

Wootton, A., 1997. *Interaction and the Development of Mind*. Cambridge University Press, Cambridge.

VI

Metalinguistic exchanges
in child language development
(with Jasper C. van den Herik)

Abstract

In everyday speech, language is often the topic of talk. In this paper we aim to draw attention to the role of such metalinguistic activity in early language development. We approach this topic through an ecological lens. To achieve this goal, we examine observational data from a single child participating in conversational episodes concerning linguistic phenomena episodes which we term "metalinguistic exchanges" – at two and three years old. We draw attention to how this child, at two years old, participates in naturally-occurring metalinguistic exchanges without yet having a productive command of metalinguistic vocabulary. The sequential organization of the metalinguistic exchanges enables her caregivers to scaffold her participation. We then compare the child's participation in metalinguistic exchanges recorded at two years old with a second set of exchanges recorded when she turned three. This comparison shows that the child's participation in metalinguistic exchanges becomes increasingly skillful and agentive as she learns to initiate metalinguistic exchanges herself. We end the paper with recommendations for future research in an ecological approach to language development. We suggest that, in order to investigate the role of metalin-

guistic activity in language development, it is crucial to look at children's increasingly skillful and agentive participation in naturally-occurring metalinguistic exchanges.

"The buildup of the first language implies an aptitude for metalingual operations." Roman Jakobson (1956/1985)

"[T]hat something can be seen in a new way is seen only when it is seen in this way." Friedrich Waismann (1968)

1. Introduction

Within everyday speech, language and linguistic actions are often the topic of talk. In Anglophone linguistic practices, for instance, we speak of language as consisting of words, meanings, sentences, and sayings; we speak of the linguistic actions of ourselves and others as referring to events and objects and ideas, telling people about things, asking and answering questions, making requests and complaints, meaning or claiming this or that, having this or that name, understanding (or not understanding) what someone says, being right or wrong; and we characterize speakers as French speakers, liars, or poets. Theorists of language have argued that metalinguistic activity is crucial for language as we know it (Hockett, 1966; Jakobson, 1956/1985; Lucy, 1993; Silverstein, 1993; Harris, 1998; Agha, 2007; Schiffrin, 1980; Dingemanse et al., 2015; Love, 1990, 2017; Taylor, 1992, 2000; van den Herik, 2017; 2019; Jones, 2017; Thibault, 2017; Duncker, 2018).

The topic of this paper is the role of metalinguistic activity in early language development. We approach this topic through an ecological lens. The ecological approach to language starts from the idea that linguistic behavior, like any other form of behavior, needs to be understood as being the situated exercise of skills (e.g. Reed, 1995; Cowley, 2011; Rietveld and Kiverstein, 2014; Baggs, 2015; Rączaszek-

Leonardi, 2016; van den Herik, 2018; Kiverstein and Van Dijk, 2021). Rather than inquiring into linguistic knowledge represented in the child's cognitive system, or abstract properties of decontextualised linguistic entities, an ecological approach to language regards it as a public activity embedded in cultural and social contexts (Fowler and Hodges, 2016).

Students of language disagree as to the role metalinguistic activity plays in early language development. On the one hand, some argue that metalinguistic skills are logically and developmentally dependent on non-reflexive linguistic skills. This view is predicated on the idea that participation in metalinguistic practices requires metalinguistic awareness, "the ability to make language forms opaque and attend to them in and for themselves", which is taken to be "a special kind of language performance, one which makes special cognitive demands, and seems to be less easily and less universally acquired than the language performances of speaking and listening" (Cazden, 1974, p. 13; cf. Hakes, 1980; Van Kleeck, 1982; Bialystok and Ryan, 1985; Cairns. 2015; Kalish, 2005; Doherty and Perner, 1998; Karmiloff-Smith, 1986; Edwards and Kirkpatrick, 1999; Rakoczy and Tomasello, 2007).[1] On the other hand, some argue that the reflexive understanding afforded by participation in metalinguistic practices is crucial for, and emerges concurrently with, children's development of linguistic abilities (e.g. Jakobson, 1956/1985; Taylor, 2010, 2011, 2013; van den Herik, 2020).

---

[1] For instance, Rakoczy and Tomasello (2007) discuss children's learning of status functions, a concept first proposed by Searle (1995): "That some X counts as a Y usually requires some way of symbolizing it as being a Y, and the default way to do this is using language to declare it a Y" (Rakoczy and Tomasello, 2007: 127). However, citing Doherty and Perner (1998), they suggest that children do not understand status functions in language until they have developed metalinguistic awareness, which, they claim is not until they are four-to-five years old.

In this paper, we aim to motivate the idea that skills for participating in metalinguistic exchanges emerge concurrently with and play a role in children's early development of linguistic abilities. To achieve this goal, we examine observational data from a single child participating in conversational episodes that we call "metalinguistic exchanges". We draw attention to how this child, at 2 years old, participates in naturally-occurring metalinguistic exchanges without yet having a productive command of metalinguistic vocabulary. The sequential organization of the metalinguistic exchanges enable her caregivers to scaffold the exchanges by initiating the metalinguistic exchange and acknowledging the child's responses as appropriate and productive contributions. We then compare the child's participation in metalinguistic exchanges recorded at 2 years old with a second set of exchanges recorded when she turned 3. This comparison shows that the child's participation in metalinguistic exchanges becomes increasingly skillful and agentive as she becomes able to initiate metalinguistic exchanges herself.

This focus on how the child's participation in metalinguistic exchanges is scaffolded can be seen as an extension of the ecological work on communicative interactions between caregiver and pre-verbal infants (e.g., Reed, 1995; Nomikou et al., 2017; Rączaszek-Leonardi, 2011, Rohlfing et al., 2020). The present work suggests that this ecological perspective on early communicative behavior can be fruitfully extended to older children that participate in metalinguistic exchanges. At the same time, this paper does not present an ecological explanation or theoretical description of the phenomenon in question. Instead, our goal is to draw attention to a phenomenon, one child's participation in metalinguistic exchanges, that is potentially of great interest both to ecological and other approaches to language development, and on this basis suggest directions for future research.

The paper is structured as follows. In Section 2 we explain how we understand the project of this paper, namely, to suggest a particular away of "looking" (Wittgenstein, 1953, §144) at the role of metalinguistic activity in early language development. We introduce the concept of metalinguistic activity and describe how our discussion of a single child's participation in naturally-occurring metalinguistic exchanges is intended to bring into view the role of metalinguistic activity in early language development. In Section 3 we ask: What does this child's participation within naturally-occurring talk about talk look like at 24 months and how does that compare to her participation in such metalinguistic talk at 36 months? We first describe the material, and then draw attention to two aspects of the child's participation in metalinguistic exchanges: first, the parents' scaffolding of her participation in the exchanges; and second, the development of her agency in metalinguistic exchanges. In Section 4, finally, we draw on this abbreviated consideration of one child's metalinguistic development to suggest some recommendations for future research on the role of metalinguistic activity in early language development.

2. Aims and method

The goal of this paper is to propose a particular "way of looking" at the role of metalinguistic activity in early language development. In doing so, we aim to draw the reader's attention to features and patterns that have usually gone unnoticed and un-researched. Our hope is that by inviting the reader to "try to look at it this way" (Taylor, 1992; Baker, 2004) we will promote the dawning of a hitherto unrecognized aspect (Wittgenstein, 1953; Waismann, 1968) of language development. The goal of this paper is determinedly not to convince the reader of any particular theoretical account of the defining properties of metalinguistic exchanges or of the role of such exchanges in language development. Instead, we take the "way of looking" presented in the paper to suggest particular questions relevant to an ecological study of metalinguistic activity and of the role of metalinguistic exchanges in early language development. We formulate these recommendations in the final section of this paper.

In line with our Wittgensteinian methodology, we introduce our topic by ostension: by drawing attention to and discussing sample instances of one child's participation in metalinguistic exchanges. We understand metalinguistic activity broadly, as referring to those instances of conversation in which language turns on itself. Our term thus includes the phenomena referenced by terms such as "metapragmatic", "metadiscursive", "metacommunicational", "metasemiotic", "metatalk", and "reflexivity". We should clarify at this point that our use of "metalinguistic activity" points to different forms of reflexivity (cf. Agha, 2007). The most perspicuous form perhaps is the use of conventional metalinguistic terms. If A says "I had a stellar time", B could ask them "what does the word 'stellar' mean?". In doing so, they rely on the conventional metalinguistic terms "word" and "mean". But they could also simply repeat the word "stellar" accompanied by a puzzled look in order to prompt A to explain what they mean. In that case, reflexive work is done without the use of conventional metalinguistic terms.

We undertake our project by discussing examples. We have limited ourselves to discussing a single child's participation in metalinguistic exchanges. The anecdotal data collected in the Appendix comes from diary notes which one of us (Talbot Taylor) compiled when his daughter Margaret was 2–2.3 years old and then again when she was 3–3.3 years old. The exchanges were selected because of their perceived metalinguistic interest. Each exchange was recorded immediately after its occurrence, either by direct written transcription or by repeating it verbatim into a smartphone, to be transcribed later.

We are acutely aware that our "verbal" presentation of the exchanges necessarily results in a limited and decontextualized perspective on the events themselves. Many aspects of the exchanges, such as the timing and prosody of the utterances, the physical circumstances in which the exchanges occurred, and the shared history of parent and child remain out of view. Accordingly, we do not present our use of the exchanges listed in the Appendix as having anything more than a pragmatic justification, enabling us to direct attention to particular aspects of parent-child metalinguistic exchanges that we will argue warrant further investigation.

The reason for having examples from both 2 and 3 years old is that some of the aspects we wish to draw attention to can best be brought out by comparing how Margaret participates in metalinguistic exchanges in different ways across these two ages. As will be evident in the paper, making this comparison is central to our project.

The data presented in this paper is limited in many ways. Margaret is just one child, raised in a middle-class American family and the daughter of two educators. Recognizing the limitations of the data discussed, we do not present our descriptions or analyses of this one child's participation in metalinguistic exchanges as generalizable to children's development of metalinguistic abilities. At the same time, the data allow us to highlight some characteristics of *this* child's skillful participation in meta-linguistic exchanges that are plausibly relevant beyond the data described.

In proposing this way of looking, we cannot escape introducing terminology to *talk about* the examples we discuss. To do so we make use of a descriptive framework. We introduce this framework as a rough-and-ready way of looking at and talking about the exchanges; we make no claims for its grounding in theory, ecological or otherwise, nor do we present the framework as the sketch of a theory of the role of metalinguistic activity in early language development. If the paper's aim of suggesting a certain way of looking at our data is achieved, then it matters little whether the descriptive framework used in achieving our aim is later modified or replaced.

At the same time, this paper was not written in a theoretical vacuum. The "way of looking" and the accompanying recommendations for research are inspired by, and can be taken up by, a wide variety research programs that study naturally occurring communicational interaction. These include, besides ecological psychology (e.g., Rączaszek-Leonardi et al., 2018; Zukow-Goldring, 1997), skilled intentionality (Van Dijk and Rietveld, 2017), conversation analysis (e.g., Schegloff 2007; Goodwin 2017), integrational linguistics (e.g., Duncker, 2018; Perregaard, 2018), linguistic anthropology (Lucy, 1993; Silverstein, 1993), discourse analysis (e.g., Schiffrin, 1980; Johnstone, 2008), interactivism (e.g., Steffensen, 2015), the distributed language perspective (e.g., Cowley, 2011; Thibault, 2011), and dialogism (e.g., Linell, 2009; Weigand, 2010). In our view the application of each of these methodologies to the study of children's participation in naturally-occurring metalinguistic activities has the potential to reveal hitherto neglected aspects of children's development and agentive uses of metalinguistic skills – and thus offer possible insight into the contribution which their emerging participatory skills within metalinguistic activities make to the expansion and refinement of their linguistic, social, and cognitive abilities through ontogeny.

3. Analysis and discussion

3.1. Introduction

In this Section, we present the data, which consists of metalinguistic exchanges between Margaret and her parents. The metalinguistic exchanges have a typical pattern, one that can best be introduced by looking at an example:

d. *(Margaret stands in front of DVD player)*
d1. Margaret: Kitty-cat. Kitty-cat.
d2. Father: You mean you want to see the kitty-cat movie?
d3. Margaret: Yah, yah.
d4. Father: Okay. But you just watched it this morning.

In this exchange, Margaret's utterance (d1) "Kitty-cat. Kitty-cat" prompts her father to initiate a metalinguistic exchange (d2) "You mean you want to see the kitty-cat movie?". Margaret responds affirmatively (d3) "Yah, yah". Note that although Margaret's response (d3) does not feature any metalinguistic terms, it is a productive and appropriate response to the metalinguistic question posed to Margaret by her father. Finally, the exchange ends with her father's utterance (d4) "Okay. But you just watched it this morning". By his response (d4), her father does (at least) two things: looking back, he acknowledges Margaret's utterance in (d3) as a productive and appropriate move in the unfolding exchange, and looking forward, he continues the interaction, moving their interaction on to the new, albeit related issue of Margaret's already having watched the movie earlier.

Many of the metalinguistic exchanges follow this pattern of exchange. In order to be able to talk about the metalinguistic exchanges, we use a few descriptive terms to refer to the different sequential components of this pattern.[2] We refer to the initial utterance, that which prompts the metalinguistic exchange and forms its topic, as the topic utterance. The

---

[2] Our descriptive terms draw inspiration from Conversation Analysis' frame-work for describing repair exchanges (Schegloff, 2007; Sidnell, 2010), al-though the metalinguistic exchanges we discuss are not limited to repair exchanges.

utterance in which the metalinguistic exchange is initiated, we call the initiation. The next utterance is the response to the initiation. We refer to the final utterance as the continuation, in order to highlight the way this utterance both brings the work of the metalinguistic exchange to a close and continues the participants' interaction into other business. Here is one more example of the sequential pattern with the descriptive terms:

a. *(Margaret and mother are sitting together in the kitchen)*
a1. Margaret: Want play with toys — *topic utterance*
a2. Mother: What did you say? — *initiation*
a3. Margaret: Play with toys. — *response*
a4. Mother: Not now. It's time for lunch — *continuation*

Although these four turns form the basic metalinguistic exchange, the exchanges can become more elaborate. Take the following example:

c. *(Margaret and father are sitting in playroom)*
c1. Margaret: Dollie — *topic utterance*
c2. Father: Which one do you want? — *initiation*
c3. Margaret: That! That one! (*Pointing at leftmost of three dolls in front of them*) — *response/topic utterance*
c4. Father: (*Holds up doll*). You mean this one? — *initiation*
c5. Margaret: Yah! — *response*
c6. Father: (*Hands doll to Margaret*) — *continuation*
c7. Margaret: (*takes doll and starts to play with it*)

This example includes two nested metalinguistic exchanges, with one utterance (c3) acting both as a response to the first exchange's initiation in (c2) and as a topic utterance prompting the initiation in (c4) of the second, nested exchange.

3.2. Metalinguistic exchanges at 2 years
Looking at the utterances that initiate the metalinguistic exchange at 2 years old, a few points stand out:

In all of the metalinguistic exchanges recorded when Margaret is 2 years old, it is always the parent, never Margaret, who initiates the metalinguistic exchanges. For example, in (d), discussed above, after Margaret says "Kitty cat. Kitty cat" while standing in front of the family DVD player, her father initiates a metalinguistic exchange in (d2) by saying "You mean you want to see the kitty-cat movie?".

A second point is that the parent initiates the metalinguistic exchange as a particular kind of metalinguistic activity. For example, in (e2) – "What did you say?" – her father asks Margaret to repeat what she just said:

b. (*Margaret brings cup to father in kitchen.*)
e1. Margaret: (*Says something indecipherable.*)   –topic utterance
e2. Father: What did you say?   – initiation
e3. Margaret: Want more milkie!   – response
e4. Father: Momma said that was enough.   – continuation
e5. Margaret: No! More!

In other exchanges initiated by the adult, Margaret is asked to clarify a particular aspect of the exchange's immediately preceding *topic utterance*. For example, in (b2) her father asks her to clarify to whom she is speaking in her pretend phone conversation.

b. (*Margaret sits with her father in the playroom*)
b1. Margaret: (*Talks on toy cellphone*)   – topic utterance
b2. Father: Who are you talking to?   – initiation
b3. Margaret: Susie   – response
b4. Father: Oh! Maybe we can go see her later.   – continuation

In example (c) printed above, her father asks Margaret to say which doll she was asking for (c2) "Which one do you want") in the request she has just made in (c1) "Dollie".

In (c4) "(*Holds up doll*) You mean this one?" and (g2) below, the parent seeks Margaret's confirmation of their expressed "candidate understanding" (Antaki, 2012) of what she said in the topic utterance. For example, while standing at the top of the stairs in (g1) Margaret says something that her mother doesn't understand. Her mother states this and then offers what she thinks Margaret may have meant, which in (g3) Margaret confirms.

g. *(Margaret stands at barrier to staircase.)*
g1. Margaret: *(Says something indecipherable.)* — *topic utterance*
g2. Mother: I don't understand. You want to go downstairs? — *initiation*
g3. Margaret: Yah. Yah. — *response*
g4. Mother: Not now, Margaret. It's time for bed. — *continuation*
g5. Margaret: *(Turns away and enters bedroom)*

In exchange (h), printed below, her father initiates first one and then a second kind of metalinguistic exchange regarding Margaret's report that she has seen a dog. Her father first asks her to confirm what she has just said, which she does in her response in (h3). He then asks her whether she has also reported this news to her mother.

h. *(Margaret turns from window to address father)*
h1. Margaret: Me see doggie. — *topic utterance*
h2. Father: No! Really? — *initiation*
h3. Margaret: Yah. Two doggie. — *response*
h4. Father: Did you tell Momma? — *continuation/initiation*
h5. Margaret: *(Turns excitedly to mother as she enters
    the room.)* See doggie! — *response*

In (f) and (i), her father's initiations have a directive character. In (f2), he tells Margaret who to address her request to and how to say it in her next turn, while in (i1) he tells her what to say: namely, to tell her sister that she 'is sorry'.

f. *(Margaret extends cup toward father who is reading)*
f1. Margaret: More! — *topic utterance*
f2. Father: Ask Momma nicely. — *initiation*

f3. Margaret: (*Turns to address mother and
       extends cup*) More please!   – *response*
f4. Mother: Good girl. (*Pours milk in cup*)   – *continuation*

Example (i) also shows the possibility of a metalinguistic exchange that is not prompted by an utterance. Instead, the topic that prompts father's initiation is a non-verbal act performed by Margaret.

i. *(Margaret pushes sister)*   – *topic*
i1. Father: Tell Cara you're sorry.   – *initiation*
i2 Margaret: *(Looks at sister.)* Sorry.   – *response*
i3. Father: Good girl. That's better.   – *continuation*

Having looked at some examples, we now zoom in on the role played by each of these sequential components of the metalinguistic exchanges. We start by discussing initiations, of which two features must be highlighted. First, initiations call on Margaret to attend to an ostended aspect of something that just happened: in particular, to an aspect of something Margaret just said (i.e., of the topic utterance) or, in the case of (i) for example, of some non-verbal-act of Margaret. We refer to this ostensive function of initiations as topicalization.

For instance, her father's question in (d) topicalizes the meaning of Margaret's immediately preceding utterance: (d2) "You mean you want to see the kitty-cat movie?". His initiation in (c2) topicalizes the referent of her request in the preceding utterance: he asks "Which one do you want?" The topic of his question in (b2) – "Who are you talking to?" – is the addressee of Margaret's talk in (b1). In both (h2) and (h4), what Margaret reports in her immediately preceding utterance is topicalized: namely, having seen dogs.

Second, the parents' initiations characterize or "typify" (Agha, 2007) the topicalized aspects of the topic utterance in one of several different culturally normative ways. That is, the initiation explicitly characterizes the topicalized aspect of the topic utterance as a matter of:

- what Margaret or someone else has said (a2, e2, e4)
- what Margaret means (c4, d2)
- what something is called (j5)
- telling someone about something (h4)
- telling someone that she is sorry (i1)
- asking someone nicely (f2)
- whom Margaret is talking to (b2)
- which one Margaret meant by what she said (c2, c4)
- being a name (j3)

We now turn attention to Margaret's responses to her parent's initiation utterances. Even though she does not use any explicitly metalinguistic expressions in her responses at 2 years old, her responses are productive and appropriate contributions to the progression of the exchange initiated by her parent. (See discussion in Section 3.4). For example, in her response to father's exchange-initiating request in (c2), asking her to specify which of her dolls she had requested in (c1), Margaret gestures in (c3) toward one doll and utters two demonstratives:

c1. Margaret: Dollie   *– topic utterance*
c2. Father: Which one do you want?   *– initiation*
c3. Margaret: That! That one!
       (*Pointing at leftmost of three dolls in front of them*)   *– response*

In (b3), responding to father's initiating query about whom she is speaking to on her toy phone, she utters the name of their next-door neighbor, "Susie".

In exchange (j) her father asks Margaret who one of her dolls is. In (j2) she tells him the doll's name. In (j3) he exclaims that the doll has the same name as Margaret herself, which she confirms in (j4).

j. *(Father and Margaret are looking at an array of dolls on
        playroom floor)*
j1. Father: Who is that? (*Points at a small doll*)   – *initiation*
j2. Margaret: Margaret   – *response*
j3. Father: Oh, but that's your name!   – *continuation/initiation*
j4. Margaret: Yah.   – *response*
j5. Father: She's called Margaret too?   – *continuation/initiation*
j6. Margaret: Yah.   – *response*
j7. Father: But Margaret has red hair.
        Your hair is brown.   – *continuation*

In exchanges (f) and (i), Margaret does what, in initiating the exchange, her father had instructed her to do. Even an affirmative response like "Yah, yah" in (d3) can be seen as a productive contribution to the exchange, given its occurrence immediately following his preceding yes-no question in (d2) and, in her father's continuation in (d4), his reply to her original request in (d1).

d1. Margaret: Kitty-cat. Kitty-cat.   – *topic utterance*
d2. Father: You mean you want to see the kitty-cat movie? – *initiation*
d3. Margaret: Yah, yah.   – *response*
d4. Father: Okay. But you just watched it this morning.   – *continuation*

As seen in (d4), the continuation contributes in various and important ways to the progression of the interaction. In the manner of the "subsequents" in Ratner and Bruner's (1978) classic analysis of communication routines or the 'acknowledge' phase in Nomikou et al.'s (2017) analysis of peekaboo games, the continuations in this data treat Margaret's response as a sequentially-appropriate and productive contribution to the exchange. In his discussion of conversational enchrony, Enfield (2013) refers to this as a "downstream interpretant" which "consummates" the preceding utterance (for a discussion on enchrony see §3.4). Our use of continuation can be distinguished from these as we use it to point both to the backward-looking acknowledgement of the previous utterance, as well as to the forward-looking continuation of the participants' unfolding interaction away from the specifically metalinguistic business of the exchange itself. The parent's continuations treat Margaret as having recognized (i) the particular kind of metalinguistic activity which the parent had initiated (requesting, directing, seeking clarification, proposing a candidate understanding, etc.), (ii) the topical focus of the exchange on a particular aspect of her topic utterance, and (iii) the particular way in which the parent's initiating utterance had typified the topical focus.

For example, in (b3), Margaret responds "Susie" to her father's initiating question in (b2) about the identity of the addressee in her toy phone conversation. Following this, his utterance in (b4) "Oh! Maybe we can go see her later" presupposes that she has correctly understood that in (b2) he had asked her to tell him the identity of her addressee in (b1) and that, in her response in (b3), she has done what he asked.

Before concluding this preliminary description of the 2- year-old exchanges, it is important to emphasize a shared general feature: they are metalinguistic exchanges. They do what we might describe as "metalinguistic work": they are reflexively and productively "directed" at—or draw attention to (van den Herik, 2018)—linguistic aspects of the activity in which Margaret and her interlocutor are currently engaged. Each is a discursive activity in which metalinguistic work is done: clarifying, correcting, confirming, requesting, directing, etc. And, although supported by parental scaffolding (discussed below), Margaret participates skillfully in these metalinguistic exchanges in ways that are suited to each exchange as initiated; and, in so doing, she contributes to the accomplishment of whatever metalinguistic work they can be said to achieve.

3.3. Metalinguistic exchanges at 3 years old

We now turn attention to Margaret's participation in metalinguistic exchanges at 3 years old. When compared to the exchanges at 2 years old, a salient feature is that around her 3rd birthday Margaret initiates several different kinds of metalinguistic exchanges.

Many of the exchanges she initiates topicalize an aspect of her interlocutor's just completed utterance. For example, in exchange (s), Margaret's mother says that it is dark outside. Then, after seeing light through the window as they go downstairs, Margaret initiates an exchange which topicalizes the truth of what her mother just said and typifies it as being "not right".

s. *(Mother and Margaret are upstairs in bedroom in the morning. Curtains are pulled. Margaret has been saying that it is light outside.)*
s1. Mother: It's still dark outside.   *– topic utterance*
(They go downstairs and see through the windows that the sun is up).
s2. Margaret: Mommy you was not right.   *– initiation*
        I was right. It not dark outside.
s3. Mother: Oh, yes. You're right. It's light now, isn't it? *– response*
s4. Margaret: Yah.   *– continuation*

In (u2), she initiates a directive exchange, topicalizing her mother's use of the expression "potty time" in (u1). She instructs her mother not to use the expression and then states that she does not want to "call" the current moment "potty time".

u. *(Mother readies Margaret to go out)*
u1. Mother: It's potty time.   *– topic utterance*
u2. Margaret: Mommy, don't say it's potty time.   *– initiation*
        I don't wanna call it potty time.
u3. Mother: Okay, but you need to go before we leave. *– response*

In (m3) Margaret objects to her mother's representation in (m2) of what she was "talking about" in (m1).

m. *(Margaret comes up to mother upset about something)*
m1. Margaret: *(says something indecipherable)*
m2. Mother: *(interrupts Margaret).*
    Why are you fidgeting?   *– topic utterance*
m3. Margaret: I not talking about that!   *– initiation*

In (n2) Margaret topicalizes her father's statement in (n1) that he would tell Momma about their seeing a rabbit while out walking, asserting that she wants to be the one to tell her.

n. *(Father and Margaret are on a short walk)*
n1. Father: I can't wait to tell Momma that we saw the rabbit. *– topic utterance*
n2. Margaret: I wanna tell Momma!   *– initiation*
n3. Father: OK. You tell her then.   *– response*
n4. *(Ten minutes later, they arrive home. Margaret speaks excitedly to mother).* We see bunny!   *– continuation*

In (q3) she topicalizes her father's attention to her utterance in (q1), complaining that he wasn't "listening", and she topicalizes his utterance in (q2), objecting that it is "not what [she] said" in (q1).

q. *(Father is washing dishes noisily in the kitchen. Margaret has been eating grapes from her bowl)*
q1. Margaret: *(Holds out empty bowl to father.)* I need nother one.
q2. Father: *(Pretending not to understand)*
    Mother's not here now.   *– topic utterance*
q3. Margaret: You not listening. That not what I said.   *– initiation*
q4. Father: It's not? I'm sorry.   *– response*
q5. Margaret: *(Holds out empty bowl)* I need nother.   *– continuation*

While in each of the examples just discussed, the metalinguistic exchange initiated by Margaret topicalizes a feature of her parent's utterance in the preceding utterance, other exchanges at 3 years topicalize something other than a previous utterance in the discursive sequence.

For instance, in (l) her father is sitting next to Margaret while she plays with a doll. Without being prompted, Margaret spontaneously declares that the name of the doll is "Margaret".

l. *(Margaret sits silently next to father and plays with tiny
       doll.)*
l1. Margaret: Her name is Margaret.   *– initiation*
l2. Father: Margaret is Cara's doll, isn't she?   *– response*
l3. Margaret: Yah.   *– continuation*

In (k) Margaret topicalizes the name of one of the pictured characters referred to in the *Winnie The Pooh* story which her father is reading to her. She interrupts his reading to point at an illustration of Eeyore and asks: "What's he called?"

k. *(Father and Margaret are looking at illustrated storybook
       together. He is reading aloud.)*
k1. Margaret: *(Pointing at figure in the book.)*
       What's he called?   *– initiation*
k2. Father: That's Eeyore.   *– response*

In (x), Margaret and her father are walking along a footpath. Margaret notices two signs along the side of the path. Without any prompting, she speculates about what the two signs "say".

(x1) Margaret: Maybe it says stop and that sign says go.   *– initiation*

Another salient feature of the 3-year-old examples is Margaret's productive use of several conventional metalinguistic expressions. She asks what someone "is called" (k1), speaks of "know[ing] what [something] is called" (v3), and declares what she wants a particular activity "[to be] called" (u2). She tells her father what a doll's "name" is (l1) and denies that what he says is "what I said" (q4). She speaks of "listening to" (q3) and "speaking to" someone (r3), of "talking about" something (m3), and she characterizes saying "one, two, three, four, five, six" as "counting" (o3). She speculates about what a sign "says" (x1) and describes her interlocutor's utterance as "teasing" (t3) and the interlocutor himself as "being funny" (t4). She speaks of "telling" someone something (n2) and of what she or her interlocutor says as being "right" or "not right" (s2). And she reports on a tv character's utterance as what he is "saying": that is, she uses "say" as a quotative before reporting the speech (p2).

As with the two-year-old exchanges, a notable feature of the metalinguistic exchanges at 3 years is the way, in their following turns, her parents treat Margaret's contributions to the exchange.

For example, in exchange (l), Margaret declares that her doll's name is "Margaret". In the next turn (l2), her father refers to the doll by that name, asking "Margaret is Cara's doll, isn't she?", which she confirms in her next turn. That is, by referring to the doll as "Margaret", he treats her as having provided metalinguistic information in (l1), namely, what the doll is called.

In (t2) and (t3) Margaret characterizes her father's utterance in (t1).

t. *(Father and Margaret are playing and tickling.)*
1. Father: I'm going to eat your toes for dinner!   – *topic utterance*
2. Margaret: *(Addressing mother.)* Daddy being funny.   – *initiation*
3. Margaret: *(Addressing father.)* You teasing!   – *initiation*
4. Father: No, I'm really going to do it!   – *response*

Her father continues the sequence in (t4) with an utterance whose expressed (albeit feigned) disagreement – "No,

I'm really going to do it" – acknowledges Margaret's metalinguistic characterizations of his (t1) utterance as non-serious.

In (n2), Margaret expresses her desire to be the one who will tell mother about seeing the rabbit, in opposition to what her father had proposed in (n1). His acceptance of this in (n3) – "OK. You tell her then" – overtly treats Margaret's (n2) as a metalinguistic objection to his utterance in (n1). In (v3), Margaret suggests that her mother may know what a flower "is called". Her father's next turn in (v4) – "OK. We'll ask her" – reflects his grasp of her utterance as such a suggestion, acknowledging it and continuing with the proposal that they ask her mother what the flower is called.

The recorded exchanges described above indicate that Margaret's skillful participation in metalinguistic exchanges develops concurrently with her development of other language skills. Margaret participates in and actively contributes to various kinds of metalinguistic activities as early as her 2nd birthday. By 3 years old, her participation in metalinguistic exchanges draws on a range of finely and conventionally articulated metalinguistic skills. In the rest of this Section we zoom in on two aspects of Margaret's participation in metalinguistic exchanges, i.e., the scaffolding provided by her caregivers and Margaret's developing metalinguistic agency. The aspects we highlight here foreshadow our discussion in Section 4 of questions and recommendations for future research on metalinguistic development.

3.4. Scaffolding

As with children's development of many other interactive and communicative skills, Margaret's increasingly skillful participation in metalinguistic exchanges is scaffolded. Scaffolding is important on two timescales (Nomikou et al., 2017). First, on the timescale of the unfolding metalinguistic exchange, Margaret's participation is facilitated and actively supported by her more competent interlocutors. Following Enfield (2013), we refer to this timescale as *enchronic*. In the words of Enfield (2013, p. 29), an "enchronic perspective on human communication focuses on sequences of interlocking or inter-dependent communicative moves". In human communication more generally, a communicative action elicits a response, where neither the initial action nor the response can be under-stood without reference to the other, according to Enfield. We use *enchronic* to highlight this intrinsically sequential charac-ter of the metalinguistic exchanges. Second, on longer time-scales, "recurring instances or features of the provided struc-ture lead to the emergence and stabilization of interaction frames that shape current and later development" (Nomikou et al., 2017: 3–4). In what follows we first take a closer look at the timescale of the exchange, and then discuss the longer timescale.

The scaffolding within the enchronic timescale is most evident in that at 2 years old, all metalinguistic exchanges are initiated by the parent. This shows a defining aspect of scaf-folding, namely its agential asymmetry (Bruner, 1983; Wil-liams, 2010). Although Margaret responds appropriately to the metalinguistic initiations of her parents, in the data at 2 years old she does not yet initiate any exchanges herself.

The scaffolding role of the parents' initiation can be seen in the fact that they call on Margaret to respond. Using Kukla and Lance's (2009, p. 138–139) term, we can say that these parental initiations have a "vocative" character. For ex-ample, in exchange (a), immediately following Margaret's "Want play with toys", her father says "What did you say?", vocatively calling on her to engage in the exchange he is initi-ating. She responds in (a3) by partially repeating what she had said in her topicalized utterance. In (h2), her father similarly elicits her participation in a metalinguistic exchange, asking her to confirm what she said in (h1), which she then does in (h3).

h1. Margaret: Me see doggie.   *– topic utterance*
h2. Father: No! Really?   *– initiation*
h3. Margaret: Yah. Two doggie.   *– response*

At the same time, such metalinguistic initiations do more than elicit any kind of response from Margaret; she is called on to respond in a way that is appropriate to the parent's initiating utterance. A further aspect of the agential asymmetry characterizing the metalinguistic exchanges at 2 years is that it is the parent, never Margaret, who topicalizes and typifies an aspect of the topic utterance: e.g., which doll she means, whom she is *speaking* to, what she *said*, how she should *ask* her mother, etc. In this way, the parent's initiation provides the topic for the metalinguistic exchange. This in turn means that Margaret's response has to relate to the typified topic if it is to be a productive contribution to the initiated exchange. Thus, while her parents' initiations do not call for Margaret to respond with specific words or phrases, they do call for responses that are appropriate to the topicalizing and typifying feature of the initiations. In other words, in addition to their asymmetrical character, the initiations also facilitate Margaret's participation in the exchanges by providing, in advance, aspects of the utterance with which Margaret will then respond.

Another important aspect of the enchronic scaffolding in the two-year-old exchanges is the parents' continuation, which does at least three things with respect to Margaret's response. First, it treats it as a response to the initiation's vocative call. Second, it treats Margaret's response as topicalizing the same aspect of her prior utterance as had been topicalized and typified by the parent. And finally, it treats her response

187

as an appropriate and productive contribution to furthering the sequential unfolding of the initiated exchange.

It is important to recognize that, even in the scaffolded exchanges at 2 years, Margaret's contribution to each metalinguistic exchange is not simply passive—it is not entirely determined by the supportive scaffolding. While the asymmetric and sequential scaffolding is crucial for the exchanges, so is Margaret's purposive and agentive contribution. For example, Margaret's response in (b3) – "Susie" – provides just that information which her father had requested by asking "Who are you talking to?" in (b2). The same applies, to a slightly lesser degree, to her response in (c3) – "That! That one!" – as well as to her replies "Margaret" in (j2), "Play with toys" in (a3), and "Yah. Two doggie" in (h3). Even a confirmatory response like "Yah, yah" in (d3) furthers the progress of the exchange and is appropriate to the initiation, which in this case was her father's yes-no question "You mean you want to see the kitty-cat movie?" in (d2). In other words, while the adult provides the scaffolding that, within the unfolding of the sequence, facilitates Margaret's productive participation within these metalinguistic exchanges at 2 years, Margaret's responses enact her understanding of the particular demand placed on her by the parent's metalinguistic initiation.

Here we can see the reciprocal relation between the scaffolding and the active participation of Margaret at 2 years. While the scaffolding is necessary for Margaret to be able to participate productively in these exchanges, her own contributions in turn enable the parental scaffolding. For example, the parent's continuation can only treat Margaret's response as an appropriate and productive contribution to the exchange because her responses are relevant to the immediately preceding initiation by the parent and its topicalizing of an aspect of her preceding utterance. At this point, Margaret has not yet mastered all the metalinguistic skills displayed by her parents, which is evidenced for example in the fact that she does not initiate metalinguistic exchanges herself. Nevertheless, because her participation is scaffolded within the enchronic timescale, she is able to actively contribute to the metalinguistic work which these exchanges accomplish.

Although the data provide no insight regarding Margaret's metalinguistic development on longer timescales, as they concern just two isolated intervals around her second and third birthdays, we can suggest a possible hypothesis concerning scaffolding on longer timescales: supported by the kind of enchronic scaffolding we have seen in the recorded exchanges with Margaret, children can become increasingly skillful and active participants in metalinguistic activities as they mature. Children's scaffolded participation within metalinguistic exchanges enables their participation in metalinguistic exchanges before they have mastered the skills to initiate them. Each metalinguistic sequence enacts—and thereby displays for the language-learner—different metalinguistic typifications of topicalized utterances. In Margaret's case, for example, by observing and participating in metalinguistic exchanges she was able to learn that the sound-pattern /mɑɹɡɹɪt/ affords being characterized as a *name*, that saying "kitty-cat" affords others asking what you mean, and that saying "Me see doggie!" affords others asking you to confirm what you say ("No! Really?").

In other words, the suggestion is that children learn what they and their interlocutors are doing with words—e.g., saying such-and-such, speaking to someone, talking about X not Y, calling something "X", etc.—in part by becoming skilled participants in sequentially-deployed metalinguistic exchanges. The enchronic scaffolding we discussed shows how metalinguistic exchanges can play this role in the child's linguistic development.

3.5. *Agency*

In comparing the metalinguistic exchanges recorded at 3 years old with those at 2 years old, one of the most salient differences is the reduction of agential asymmetry.

As we saw in Section 3.3, the 3-year-old exchanges include examples in which Margaret vocatively initiates exchanges and topicalizes, as well as conventionally typifies, aspects of utterances. By focusing on her active role in metalinguistic exchanges, we draw attention to ways that at least part of Margaret's developing communicational proficiency has a metalinguistic character. In other words, Margaret's increasingly skillful participation in metalinguistic exchanges contributes to her developing agency. While it is not our aim to sketch a theory of agency here, we do want to draw attention to what Margaret, at 3 years, is able to achieve by means of her skillful participation in metalinguistic exchanges.

In line with the discussion of enchrony in the previous subsection, we can see that Margaret's skillful participation in metalinguistic activities is woven into unfolding sequential exchanges. Her contributions to the metalinguistic exchanges have a Janus-like character, facing backward as well as forward. Al-though utterances in the enchronic frame of dialogue always have both retrospective and prospective aspects, it is often the case that, in Margaret's utterances at 2 years old, one aspect is more pronounced. First, let us look at utterances that primarily look back.

Looking back, Margaret's utterances retrospectively typify the utterances of herself and those of others. For example, in exchange (s) Margaret's mother says that it is still dark outside. In (s2) Margaret initiates the metalinguistic exchange, first claiming that her mother was "not right" and that she was "right". Here she uses conventional metalinguistic vocabulary to typify the correctness of both the topic utterance and of her own earlier utterance. In her response in (s3), her mother signals her acceptance of Margaret's metalinguistic claims: "Oh, yes. You're right." Finally, Margaret's continuation in (s4), "Yah", acknowledges that she is satisfied with her mother's response.

Margaret can also typify other aspects of her communicative behavior. In exchange (r), for example, her initiation (r3) "I not speaking to you" typifies the addressee of the topic utterance (r1) "No, no tights" as not her father.

r. *(Mother, father, and Margaret are in Margaret's bedroom.*
       Mother holds out tights to Margaret.)
1. Margaret: *(Speaking to mother)* No, no tights.
2. Father: *(Speaking to Margaret)*
       It's supposed to be colder today.   – *topic utterance*
3. Margaret: *(Addressing father)* I not speaking to you. – *initiation*
4. Father: Oh, well, excuse me then.   – *response*

A third example can be found in exchange (q). Here Margaret, after eating some grapes, says (q1) "I need nother one". Her father, in response, pretends not to understand by saying (q2) "Mother's not here now". This utterance prompts Margaret to initiate a metalinguistic exchange by saying in (q3) "You not listening. That not what I said". Margaret thus first typifies her father's behavior as "not listening" during the remark she addressed to him in (q1); he has failed to pay proper attention to what she was saying. She then characterizes her father's utterance in (q2) as "not being what I said". In response, her father excuses himself, after which Margaret repeats her original utterance (q1), by saying (q5) "I need nother".

Although these three examples first and foremost have a retrospective orientation, they also prospectively shape in part how the exchange unfolds. Here, once more, it is important to see the place which Margaret's utterances occupy within the sequential context of the unfolding exchanges. In exchange (s) Margaret's claim that her mother was not right, and the mother's response that acknowledges this fact, together imply that the participants now agree that it is light outside. This consensus draws the earlier disagreement to a close such that the conversation can now continue in a different direction. In a second example, by saying (r3) "I not speaking to you", Margaret expresses her intention not to reply to her father's preceding utterance, but to continue the exchange with her mother. Finally, in exchange (q), Margaret's remark (q4) "That not what I said", together with her father's acknowledgement in his response, establishes the fact that her father misheard and opens up the possibility for Margaret to repeat her initial utterance.

Let us now turn attention to her utterances at 3 years whose prospective character is more salient. These utterances enable Margaret to creatively redirect an ongoing exchange. For example, in (n) her father says that he (n1) "can't wait" to tell mother the news that they have seen a rabbit. In her initiation, Margaret objects (n2) "I wanna tell Momma!" and in so doing prospectively directs the topical focus of the sequence to one of several metalinguistic typifications afforded by her father's immediately preceding utterance. That is, in (n2) she explicitly topicalizes the issue, not of *what* news will be told or *to whom* it will be told, or even *whether* it will be told, but of *who* will do the "telling". Her father's utterance in (n3) then continues the sequence in the direction she has initiated, indexing in (n4) his acceptance of her expressed desire to be the one to tell the news to her mother.

In exchange (v), printed below, Margaret utters a nonsense word in (v2) when her father asks her what a flower is called in (v1). But in (v3), she prospectively redirects the exchange from a question addressed to *her* about the flower's name to a question concerning her mother's knowledge of the flower's name. She suggests that her mother might, as she says, "know what it's called". In (v4) her father continues the sequence in the direction she has taken it, proposing that they ask mother on their return home.

v. (*Margaret and father walk through the fields*)
1. Father: (*Points at wildflower.*) What's that called?   – *topic utterance*
2. Margaret: I call that a (*produces indecipherable nonsense
         word and laughs*).
3. Margaret: (*Short pause.*)
         Maybe Mommy know what it's called.   – *initiation*
4. Father: OK. We'll ask her.   – *response*

Whereas in exchanges (n) and (v), Margaret's initiation is prompted by something her father just said, there are also exchanges in which Margaret's initiation does not topicalize a previous utterance by her parent. For example, in exchange (l), Margaret plays with a doll, and informs her father that (l1) "Her name is Margaret".

In addition to using metalinguistic utterances to provide information, Margaret can also use them to request information. In exchange (k), Margaret points at a figure in a book and asks her father (k1) "What's he called?". In his response, her father provides the requested information by saying (k2) "That's Eeyore". Finally, in exchange (x), Margaret speculates on what two signs mean that she and her father come across during a short walk: (x1) "Maybe it says stop and that sign says go".

In sum, at 3 years old we observe Margaret skillfully and agentively contributing to metalinguistic exchanges. Whereas at 2 years old her participation is limited to responding to her parents' initiations, we can see that at 3 years old Margaret initiates and otherwise contributes to metalinguistic exchanges in an active and creative way. In so doing, she contributes to the retrospective determination of the communicational import of her own and her interlocutors' utterances, as well as to the prospective shaping of the subsequent progression of the metalinguistic exchanges in which she is engaged.

4. Recommendations for research

We are well aware that the conclusions which we have proposed regarding Margaret's metalinguistic development cannot justifiably be generalized to other children, let alone to the abstraction named "the child". Indeed, we caution against taking it for granted that, in addressing the questions we pose below, research on one child or a population of children will yield answers that apply beyond that particular child or population of children (Schieffelin and Ochs, 1984). The more reasonable assumption is that the development, social scaffolding, and agentive use of metalinguistic skills—as well as what the skills are that are acquired—will vary across communities and languages, even greatly. It should not be assumed that metalinguistic development proceeds in a uniform fashion or direction, or even toward commensurate outcomes, within or between different cultural-linguistic communities and social environments (Agha, 2007; Taylor, 2012).

We do believe, however, that the data discussed in Section 3 justify the hypothesis that much could be learned from an ecologically-focused study of children's developing participatory skills within metalinguistic exchanges. We therefore feel that our observations regarding the role of metalinguistic activity in some scenes in this one child's early language development motivate recommendations regarding new research questions and research methods that merit exploration in future research on language development, not only during this early period but throughout ontogeny. Fleshing out these recommendations is the aim of the current section.

The recorded exchanges show that at 2 years old Margaret already participates productively in metalinguistic exchanges with her parents, albeit with limited skill. Margaret's participatory skills and agency within various metalinguistic activities did not emerge all at once but were gradually refined and expanded over time. Take the example of exchanges concerning repeating something that has been said. At 2 years old, when a parent asks her to repeat what *she* has said, she does so, as in exchanges (a) and (e); yet, at 3 years old, she is observed repeating what *someone else* has said, as in exchange (p). Similarly, while at 2 years old she replies "Yah" to her father's exchange-initiating question about the truth of what she has just said in exchange (h), at 3 years we find Margaret herself initiating a similar exchange in (s), in which the topic concerns whether it is what she said or what her mother said that is true. Two questions which ecological studies of linguistic development should therefore be expected to address are:

- At what age do the children studied begin to participate in metalinguistic exchanges with their caregivers and peers?

- What refinement and expansion of the children's skillful and agentive participation participatory skills in metalinguistic exchanges can be observed as they develop through ontogeny?

Margaret's earliest participation in metalinguistic exchanges was facilitated by parental scaffolding within the exchanges' sequentially unfolding framework. By 3 years old she was participating with greater agency in metalinguistic exchanges. This suggests the following questions for future research:

- Is the children's participation within early metalinguistic exchanges facilitated by more competent peers and caregivers? If so, what scaffolding patterns can be observed?

- Over the longer timescales of ontogeny, when and in what ways does the children's engagement in metalinguistic exchanges display increasing agency?

Here we note that our discussion of the scaffolding and growing agency of the child is in line with existing ecological approaches to the development of communicative and linguistic skills. Think for example of Reed (1995), who argues that a Field of Promoted Action which is sustained by the scaffolding of caregivers and siblings is vital for understanding the development of skill, including linguistic skills. Reed describes actions that were first in the Field of Promoted Action and transfer over time to the Field of Free Action. This accords with our description of Margaret's development, whose participation in metalinguistic exchanges is at 2 years old dependent on the parent's scaffolding, while at 3 years old she is able to freely initiate metalinguistic exchanges herself. Moreover, our discussion of scaffolding and agency agrees with ecological work on the emergence of early communicative behavior (e.g., Reed, 1995; Nomikou et al., 2017; Rączaszek-Leonardi et al., 2013, Rohlfing et al., 2020). Our discussion of how Margaret participates in metalinguistic exchanges suggests that the ecological perspective can be fruitfully applied to older children and to sophisticated linguistic skills.

At the same time, we suggest that the study of metalinguistic exchanges might be a crucial element in extending the ecological study of children's developing skills in "doing things with words" (Rączaszek-Leonardi, 2009, p. 662). The recorded exchanges show that Margaret's increasingly proficient participatory skills within metalinguistic activities allow her to be a more resourceful, adroit, and agentive contributor to the co-construction of communicative interactions. For instance, she is able, in concert with her interlocutors, to contribute more effectually to the sequential and collaborative determination of what she did or did not say, whom her utterances were or were not addressed to, what her utterances were 'about', what her utterances meant or didn't mean, etc. As she gets older, Margaret is also able to contribute with greater skill to the sequential and collaborative determination of what her interlocutors or 3rd persons said and what they meant, the kind of communicative acts her interlocutors have performed (teasing, listening, etc.), whether her interlocutors have or have not understood her, whether what her interlocutor said was 'right' or not, etc. Developing the skills for engaging in metalinguistic exchanges are among those required for keeping such languaging affordances "available" in our communicational practices. Moreover, we see her making use of her metalinguistic skills to prospectively direct ongoing communicational activities towards the achievement of her various ends: e.g., to avoid having to wear tights, to express her displeasure with her interlocutor, to follow a picture-book story, to be the one who gets to tell mother the news, to make her father to respond seriously to her request to put more grapes in her bowl, and so on. Future research on (meta)-linguistic development should then address the following questions:

- In what ways are the children observed to make use of their developing metalinguistic skills to further their communicational ends within the dynamic unfolding of dialogic interactions?

- How does the emergence and subsequent elaboration of the children's participatory skills within metalinguistic activities correlate with and contribute to the development of their abilities and agency within other forms of linguistic, social, and cognitive activities?

In addition to the particular research questions proposed above, we also suggest that ecological research on metalinguistic development consider the following two methodological recommendations.

We first note that Margaret's developing metalinguistic skills were observed to emerge in two-person communicative interactions: that is, in the back-and-forth, sequentially-unfolding exchanges. She first was seen to contribute to the sequential unfolding of metalinguistic exchanges at 2 years old, not by uttering any conventional metalinguistic expressions, but rather by her responsive behavior in the turns immediately following her interlocutors' metalinguistic initiations. If we had limited our observations only to taking note of Margaret's production of conventional metalinguistic expressions in the exchanges at two- or even 3-years old, then nearly all of what those observations reveal about her developing metalinguistic skills would then have been invisible. Accordingly, we recommend that research on the development of metalinguistic skills in ontogeny should not restrict its focus to the acquisition and use by children of a narrow set of canonical metalinguistic expressions, whether these are the conventional expressions of a particular language community or the terms for metalinguistic concepts which, for theoretical reasons, are assumed to be cognitive universals (e.g., Pinker, 1994; Wierzbicka, 2001). Instead, such research should broaden its focus to include the role of children's contributions—both verbal and nonverbal, and responsive as well as productive—within the turn-by-turn sequential unfolding of naturally-occurring metalinguistic exchanges.

Second, in line with the first recommendation, our observations also suggest that greater research attention should be given to how the children's interlocutors respond to the children's contributions in the turns we have termed continuations. For example, in the exchanges at 2 years old, it was only by observing how her parents continued immediately following Margaret's responses to their metalinguistic initiations that the contribution made by her responses to the unfolding of each of the metalinguistic exchanges was identifiable. At the same time, and for the same reason, research attention should be given to the responses uttered by children's interlocutors when, as Margaret was observed to do at 3 years old, the children themselves initiate metalinguistic exchanges and, in so doing, topicalize and typify aspects of sequentially preceding or following utterances.

5. Conclusion

This paper has presented a way of "looking at" one child's development of metalinguistic skills: namely, in terms of her increasingly skillful participation in and agentive contribution to naturally-occurring metalinguistic exchanges. What we were thus able to see in Section 3 was made possible by foregrounding the integration of the recorded exchanges within interactionally-situated, sequentially-unfolding, dialogic contexts. This way of "looking at" Margaret's development of metalinguistic skills at two and 3 years old suggests:

(i) that her metalinguistic skills developed as a participant *within* such dialogic contexts;

(ii) that her increasingly skillful participation within metalinguistic activities was *facilitated* by her more competent interlocutors acting within the sequentially-progressive character of such contexts;

(iii) that her metalinguistic skills were developed *for* participating in and agentively contributing to the dynamic unfolding of such dialogic contexts; and

(iv) that ecological research on language development should
     devote attention to children's evolving participation
     within and contribution to naturally-occurring metalin-
     guistic exchanges occurring within such dialogic con-
     texts.

Margaret's development of metalinguistic skills ap-
peared first in her sequential responses to her interlocutors'
metalinguistic utterances and then, little by little, in her own
initiations of and agency within metalinguistic exchanges. Her
metalinguistic skills developed gradually during the period
from which the diary examples are chosen. They continue to
do so today at 12 years old. The combined effect of literacy
training and the discursive environment of schooling, including the new forms of social scaffolding provided by the latter,
has been adding to and transforming her metalinguistic know-
how in innumerable ways – at times, it would seem, on a daily
basis. She makes active and creative use of her continuously
developing metalinguistic skills and techniques in her contributions to communicative interactions with interlocutors of all
ages, as well as in the way she herself scaffolds the participation of much younger friends and relations within metalinguistic activities. It is clear that her development of metalinguistic
skills has not been a matter of sudden illumination. Her metalinguistic development has proceeded in a piecemeal way, advancing at a variable rate through the ever-increasing motley
of language-games and other assorted communicative activities in which she comes to participate. While, at a given time
in this development, she may have known how to engage met-
alinguistically within certain language-games (e.g., talking
about what people, animals, and dolls are called), she will not
yet have known how to do so in other language-games (e.g.,
explaining why she said something or what someone was suggesting). The elaboration of her metalinguistic skills—and

thus of her language abilities and agency—continues in this gradual and piecemeal way through her school years today.

In the background of the present paper lurks a broader question: will ecological psychology, originally developed as a theory of visual perception by Gibson (1979), be able to explain human linguistic behavior and language development? In this paper we have suggested a way of looking at an important aspect of one child's language development in terms of her increasingly skillful and agentive participation in metalinguistic exchanges. In so doing, we hope to have provided an illustrative example of an analytical approach which is compatible with the ecological perspective.

Funding

Talbot Taylor was supported by research funding from the College of William and Mary. Jasper van den Herik was supported by the European Research Council (ERC Starting Grant 679190 (EU Horizon 2020) for the Project AFFORDS-HIGHER awarded to Erik Rietveld).

Acknowledgements

We are grateful to two reviewers, to Leslie Cochrane, Kate Harrigan, and Dorthe Duncker, who read an early version of the manuscript, to the Embodied Cognition Reading Group (Amsterdam), to the editors of the special issue Catherine Read, Nancy Rader, and Joanna Rączaszek-Leonardi, and, of course, to Margaret Taylor.

Appendix
Metalinguistic exchanges at 2.0–2.3 years

a. *(Margaret and mother are sitting together in the kitchen)*
1. Margaret: Want play with toys
2. Mother: What did you say?
3. Margaret: Play with toys.

4. Mother: Not now. It's time for lunch.

b. *(Margaret sits with her father in the playroom)*
1. Margaret: *(Talks on toy cellphone)*
2. Father: Who are you talking to?
3. Margaret: Susie
4. Father: Oh! Maybe we can go see her later.

c. *(Margaret and father are sitting in playroom)*
1. Margaret: Dollie
2. Father: Which one do you want?
3. Margaret: That! That one! *(Pointing at leftmost of three dolls in front of them)*
4. Father: *(Holds up doll).* You mean this one?
5. Margaret: Yah!
6. Father: *(Hands doll to Margaret)*
7. Margaret: *(takes doll and starts to play with it)*

d. *(Margaret stands in front of DVD player)*
1. Margaret: Kitty-cat. Kitty-cat.
2. Father: You mean you want to see the kitty-cat movie?
3. Margaret: Yah, yah.
4. Father: Okay. But you just watched it this morning.

e. *(Margaret brings cup to father in kitchen.)*
1. Margaret: *(Says something indecipherable.)*
2 Father: What did you say?
3. Margaret: Want more milkie!
4. Father: Momma said that was enough.
5. Margaret: No! More!

f. *(Margaret extends cup toward father who is reading)*
1. Margaret: More!
2. Father: Ask Momma nicely.

3. Margaret: *(Turns to address mother and extends cup)*
    More please!
4. Mother: Good girl. *(Pours milk in cup)*

g. *(Margaret stands at barrier to staircase.)*
1. Margaret: *(Says something indecipherable.)*
2. Mother: I don't understand. You want to go downstairs?
3. Margaret: Yah. Yah.
4. Mother: Not now, Margaret. It's time for bed.
5. Margaret: *(Turns away and enters bedroom)*

h. *(Margaret turns from window to address father)*
1. Margaret: Me see doggie.
2. Father: No! Really?
3. Margaret: Yah. Two doggie.
4. Father: Did you tell Momma?
5. Margaret: *(Turns excitedly to mother as she enters the
    room.)* See doggie!

i. *(Margaret pushes sister)*
1. Father: Tell Cara you're sorry.
2. Margaret: *(Looks at sister.)* Sorry.
3. Father: Good girl. That's better.

j. *(Father and Margaret are looking at an array of dolls on
    playroom floor)*
1. Father: Who is that? *(Points at a small doll)*
2. Margaret: Margaret
3. Father: Oh, but that's your name!
4. Margaret: Yah.
5. Father: She's called Margaret too?
6. Margaret: Yah.
7. Parent: But Margaret has red hair. Your hair is brown.

Metalinguistic exchanges at 3.0–3.3 years
k. *(Father and Margaret are looking at illustrated storybook together. He is reading aloud.)*
1. Margaret: *(Pointing at figure in the book.)* What's he called?
2. Father: That's Eeyore.
l. *(Margaret sits silently next to father and plays with tiny doll.)*
1. Margaret: Her name is Margaret.
2. Father: Margaret is Cara's doll, isn't she?
3. Margaret: Yah.

m. *(Margaret comes up to mother upset about something)*
1. Margaret: *(says something indecipherable)*
2. Mother: *(interrupts Margaret).* Why are you fidgeting?
3. Margaret: I not talking about that!

n. *(Father and Margaret are on a short walk)*
1. Father: I can't wait to tell Momma that we saw the rabbit.
2. Margaret: I wanna tell Momma!
3. Father: OK. You tell her then.
4. *(Ten minutes later, they arrive home. Margaret speaks excitedly to mother).* We see bunny!

o. *(Margaret is sitting on toilet)*
1. Margaret: One, two, three, four, five, six.
2. Father: What are you doing?
3. Margaret: I counting before the peepee come out.
4. Father: Oh. How many does it take?

p. *(Father and Margaret are watching television. Cartoon character sings)*
1. Father: What's he doing?
2. Margaret: He saying 'I'm the map. I'm the map.'

q. *(Father is washing dishes noisily in the kitchen. Margaret has been eating grapes from her bowl)*
1. Margaret: *(Holds out empty bowl to father.)* I need nother one.
2. Father: *(Pretending not to understand)* Mummy's not here now.
3. Margaret: You not listening. That not what I said.
4. Father: It's not? I'm sorry.
5. Margaret: *(Holds out empty bowl)* I need nother.

r. *(Mother, father, and Margaret are in Margaret's bedroom. Mother holds out tights to Margaret.)*
1. Margaret: *(Speaking to mother)* No, no tights.
2. Father: *(Speaking to Margaret)* It's supposed to be colder today.
3. Margaret: *(Addressing father)* I not speaking to you.
4. Father: Oh, well, excuse me then.

s. *(Mother and Margaret are upstairs in bedroom in the morning. Curtains are pulled. Margaret has been saying that it is light outside.)*
1. Mother: It's still dark outside.
(They go downstairs and see through the windows that the sun is up).
2. Margaret: Mommy you was not right. I was right. It not dark outside.
3. Mother: Oh, yes. You're right. It's light now, isn't it?
4. Margaret: Yah.

t. *(Father and Margaret are playing and tickling.)*
1. Father: I'm going to eat your toes for dinner!
2. Margaret: *(Addressing mother.)* Daddy being funny.
3. Margaret: *(Addressing father.)* You teasing!
4. Father: No, I'm really going to do it!

u. *(Mother readies Margaret to go out)*
1. Mother: It's potty time.
2. Margaret: Mommy, don't say it's potty time. I don't wanna call it potty time.
3. Mother: Okay, but you need to go before we leave.

v. *(Margaret and father walk through the fields)*
1. Father: *(Points at wildflower.)* What's that called?
2. Margaret: I call that a *(produces indecipherable nonsense word and laughs).*
3. Margaret: *(Short pause.)* Maybe Mommy know what it's called.
4. Father: OK. We'll ask her.

w. *(Margaret sitting near open window and hears birds singing. Addresses father.)*
1. Margaret: Guess what?
2. Father: What?
3. Margaret: Birdy say 'Tweet tweet'.
4. Father: That's a catbird, I think.

x. *(Father and Margaret are walking together. Margaret sees red and green signs by side of the footpath.)*
1. Margaret: Maybe it says stop and that sign says go.

References

Agha, A., 2007. *Language and Social Relations*. Cambridge University Press, Cambridge.

Antaki, C., 2012. Affiliative and disaffiliative candidate understandings. *Discourse Studies* 14 (5), 531–547.

Baggs, E., 2015. A radical empiricist theory of speaking: linguistic meaning without conventions. *Ecological Psychology* 27 (3), 251–264. https://doi.org/10.1080/10407413.2015.1068655.

Baker, G.P., 2004. *Wittgenstein's Method: Neglected Aspects*. Blackwell, Oxford.

Bialystok, E., Bouchard-Ryan, E., 1985. Toward a definition of metalinguistic skill. *Merrill-Palmer Quarterly*. 31 (3), 229–251.

Bruner, J., 1983. *Child's Talk: Learning to Use Language*. Oxford University Press, Oxford.

Cairns, H., 2015. Metalinguistic skills of children. In: Becker, M., Grinstead, J., Rothman, J. (Eds.), *Generative Linguistics and Acquisition*. John Benjamins Publishing Company, pp. 271–290.

Cazden, C.B., 1974. Play with language and metalinguistic awareness: one dimension of language experience. *International Journal of Early Childhood* 6 (12), 12–23.

Cowley, S.J., 2011. Distributed language. In: Cowley, S. (Ed.), *Distributed Language*. John Benjamins, Amsterdam/ Philadelphia, pp. 185–210.

Dingemanse, M., Roberts, S.G., Baranova, J., Blythe, J., Drew, P., Floyd, S., Gisladottir, R.S., Kendrick, K.H., Levinson, S.C., Manrique, E., Rossi, R., Enfield, N.J., 2015. Universal principles in the repair of communication problems. *PLoS One* 10 (9), 1–15. https://doi.org/10.1371/journal.pone.0136100.

Doherty, M., Perner, J., 1998. Metalinguistic awareness and theory of mind: just two words for the same thing? *Cognitive Development* 13, 279–305.

Duncker, D., 2018. Sign making in dialogue. *Language and Dialogue* 8 (1), 139–158.

Edwards, H., Kirkpatrick, A., 1999. Metalinguistic awareness in children: a developmental progression. *Journal of Psycholinguistic Research* 28, 313–329.

Enfield, N., 2013. *Relationship Thinking*. Oxford UP, Oxford.

Fowler, C.A., Hodges, B.H., 2016. Finding common ground: alternatives to code models for language use. *New Ideas in Psychology* 42, 1–6. https://doi.org/10.1016/j.newideapsych.2016.03.001.

Gibson, J.J., 1979. *The Ecological Approach to Visual Perception*. Houghton-Mifflin, Boston.

Goodwin, C., 2017. *Co-operative Action*. Cambridge UP, Cambridge.

Hakes, D.T., 1980. *The Development of Metalinguistic Abilities in Children*. Springer, Berlin.

Harris, R., 1998. *Introduction to Integrational Linguistics*. Pergamon, Oxford.

Hockett, C., 1966. The problem of universals in language. In: Greenberg, J. (Ed.), *Universals of Language*. M.I.T. Press, Cambridge, Mass.

Jakobson, R., 1956/1985. Metalanguage as a linguistic problem. In his: *Selected Writings*, VII. Ed. S. Rudy., The Hague, Mouton.

Johnstone, B., 2008. *Discourse Analysis*. Blackwell, Oxford.

Jones, P.E., 2017. Language – the transparent tool: reflections on reflexivity and instrumentality. *Language Sciences* 61, 5–16. https://doi.org/10.1016/j.langsci.2016.09.011

Kalish, C.W., 2005. Becoming status conscious: children's appreciation of social reality. *Philosophical Explorations* 8, 245–263.

Karmiloff-Smith, 1986. From meta-processes to conscious access: evidence from children's metalinguistic and repair data. *Cognition* 23 (2), 95–147.

Kiverstein, J., Van Dijk, L., 2021. Language without representation: Gibson's first- and second-hand perception on a pragmatic continuum. *Language Sciences* 85, 101380. https://doi.org/10.1016/j.langsci.2021.101380.

Kukla, R., Lance, M., 2009. *'Yo!' and 'Lo!': The Pragmatic Topography of the Space of Reasons.* Harvard UP, Cambridge.

Linell, Per, 2009. *Rethinking Language, Mind and World Dialogically.* Information Age Publishing.

Love, N., 1990. The locus of languages in a redefined linguistics. In: Davis, H.G., Taylor, T.J. (Eds.), *Redefining Linguistics.* Routledge, London/New York, pp. 53–118.

Love, N., 2017. On languaging and languages. *Language Sciences* 61, 113–147. https://doi.org/10.1016/j.langsci.2017.04.001.

Lucy, J.A., 1993. General introduction. In: Lucy, J.A. (Ed.), *Reflexive language: Reported Speech and Metapragmatics.* Cambridge University Press, pp. 1–4.

Nomikou, I., Leonardi, G., Radkowska, A., Rączaszek-Leonardi, J., Rohlfing, K., 2017. Taking up an active role: emerging participation in early mother–infant interaction during peekaboo routines. *Frontiers in Psychology* 8, 1656 https://doi.org/10.3389/fpsyg.2017.01656.

Perregaard, B., 2018. The dynamics of interactional and intentional pattern formation in children's language

socialization. *Language & Communication* 62/A, 39-
50.

Pinker, S., 1994. *The Language Instinct*. William Morrow,
New York.

Rączaszek-Leonardi, J., 2009. Symbols as constraints: the
structuring role of dynamics and self-organization in
natural language. *Pragmatics & Cognition* 17 (3),
653–676. https://doi.org/10.1075/pc.17.3.09ras.

Rączaszek-Leonardi, J., 2011. Language as a system of
replicable constraints. In: Pattee, H. (Ed.), *Laws,
Language and Life: Howard Pattee's Classic Papers
on the Physics of Symbols*. Springer, Dordrecht,
p.295-333.

Rączaszek-Leonardi, J., 2016. How does a word become a
message? An illustration on a developmental timescale. *New Ideas in Psychology* 42, 46–55.
https://doi.org/10.1016/j.newideapsych.2015.08.001.

Rączaszek-Leonardi, J., Nomikou, I., Rohlfing, K.J., 2013.
Young children's dialogical actions: the beginnings of
purposeful intersubjectivity. *IEEE Transactions
on Autonomous Mental Development* 5 (3), 210–221.
https://doi.org/10.1109/TAMD.2013.2273258.

Rączaszek-Leonardi, J., Nomikou, I., Rohlfing, K.J., Deacon,
T.W., 2018. Language development from an ecological perspective: ecologically valid ways to abstract
symbols. *Ecological Psychology* 30 (1), 39–73.
https://doi.org/10.1080/10407413.2017.1410387.

Rakoczy, H., Tomasello, M., 2007. The ontogeny of social
ontology: steps to shared intentionality and status
functions. In: Tsohatzidis, S.L. (Ed.), *Intentional
Acts and Institutional Facts*. Springer, Dordrecht.

Ratner, N., Bruner, J., 1978. Games, social exchange and the
acquisition of language. *Journal of Child Language* 5
(3), 391–401.

Reed, E.S., 1995. The ecological approach to language development: a radical solution to Chomsky's and Quine's problems. *Language & Communication* 15 (1), 1–29. https://doi.org/10.1016/0271-5309(94)E0010-9.

Rietveld, E., Kiverstein, J., 2014. A rich landscape of affordances. *Ecological Psychology* 26 (4), 325–352. https://doi.org/10.1080/10407413.2014.958035.

Rohlfing, Katharina J., Leonardi, Giuseppe, Nomikou, Iris, Rączaszek-Leonardi, Joanna, Hüllermeier, Eyke, 2020. Multimodal turn-taking: motivations, methodological challenges, and novel approaches. *IEEE Transactions on Cognitive and Developmental Systems*, 12 (2). https://doi.org/10.1109/TCDS.2019.2892991.

Schegloff, E., 2007. *Sequence Organization in Interaction. A Primer in Conversation Analysis I*. Cambridge UP, Cambridge.

Schieffelin, B., Ochs, E., 1984. Language acquisition and socialization: three developmental stories and their implications. In: Shweder, R., Levine, R. (Eds.), *Culture Theory: Essays on Mind, Self and Emotion*. Cambridge University Press, pp. 276–320.

Schiffrin, D., 1980. Meta-talk: organizational and evaluative brackets in discourse. *Sociological Inquiry* 50 (3-4), 199–236.

Searle, J., 1995. *The Construction of Social Reality*. The Free Press, New York.

Sidnell, J., 2010. *Conversation Analysis: An Introduction*. Wiley-Blackwell, West Sussex.

Silverstein, M., 1993. Metapragmatic discourse and metapragmatic function. In: Lucy, J.A. (Ed.), *Reflexive Language: Reported Speech and Metapragmatics*. Cambridge University Press.

Steffensen, Sune V., 2015. Distributed Language and Dialogism: notes on non-locality, sense-making and interactivity. *Language Sciences* 50, 105–119.

Taylor, T., 1992. *Mutual Misunderstanding*. Duke UP, Durham, N.C./Routledge, London.

Taylor, T.J., 2000. Language constructing language: the implications of reflexivity for linguistic theory. *Language Sciences* 22, 483–499. https://doi.org/10.1016/S0388-0001(00)00016-4.

Taylor, T.J., 2010. Where does language come from? The role of reflexive enculturation in language development. Language Sciences 32, 14–27. https://doi.org/10.1016/j.langsci.2008.12.014.

Taylor, T.J., 2011. Language development and the integrationist. *Language Sciences* 33, 579–583. https://doi.org/10.1016/j.langsci.2011.04.029.

Taylor, T.J., 2012. Understanding others and understanding language: how do children do it? *Language Sciences* 34, 1–12 https://doi.org/10.1016/j.langsci.2011.07.001.

Taylor, T.J., 2013. Calibrating the child for language: Meredith Williams on a Wittgensteinian approach to language socialization. *Language Sciences* 40, 308–320. https://doi.org/10.1016/j.langsci.2013.07.002.

Thibault, P.J., 2011. First-order languaging dynamics and second-order language: the distributed language view. *Ecological Psychology* 23, 1–36. https://doi.org/10.1080/10407413.2011.591274.

Thibault, P.J., 2017. The reflexivity of human languaging and Nigel Love's two orders of language. *Language Sciences* 61, 74–85. https://doi.org/10.1016/j.langsci.2016.09.014.

van den Herik, J.C., 2017. Linguistic know-how and the orders of language. *Language Sciences*, 17–27. https://doi.org/10.1016/j.langsci.2016.09.009765.

van den Herik, J.C., 2019. *Talking about Talking: An Ecological-Enactive Perspective on Language* (Unpublished doctoral dissertation). Erasmus University Rotterdam, Faculty of Philosophy.

van den Herik, J.C., 2018. Attentional actions: an ecological-enactive account of utterances of concrete words. *Psychology of Language and Communication* 22 (1), 90–123. https://doi.org/10.2478/plc-2018-0005.

van den Herik, J.C., 2020. Rules as resources: an ecological-enactive perspective on linguistic normativity. *Phenomenology and the Cognitive Sciences* https://doi.org/10.1007/s11097-020-09676-0.

Van Dijk, L., Rietveld, E., 2017. Foregrounding socio-material practice in our understanding of affordances: the skilled intentionality framework. *Frontiers in Psychology* 7, 1969. https://doi.org/10.3389/fpsyg.2016.01969.

Van Dijk, L., Rietveld, E., 2021. Situated talking. *Language Sciences* 87, 1–14. https://doi.org/10.1016/j.langsci.2021.101389.

Van Kleeck, A., 1982. The emergence of linguistic awareness: a cognitive framework. *Merrill-Palmer Quarterly* 28 (2), 237–265.

Waismann, F., 1968. *How I See Philosophy*. Palgrave Macmillan, London.

Weigand, E., 2010. *Dialogue – the Mixed Game*. John Benjamins, Amsterdam.

Wierzbicka, A., 2001. Comments. *Current Anthropology* 42 (4), 506–507.

Williams, M., 2010. *Blind Obedience: Paradox and Learning in the Later Wittgenstein*. Routledge, London.

Wittgenstein, L., 1953/2009. *Philosophical Investigations* (Revised, fourth ed.) Wiley-Blackwell, Oxford.

Zukow-Goldring, P., 1997. A social ecological realist approach to the emergence of the lexicon: educating attention to amodal invariants in gesture and speech. In: Dent-Read, C., Zukow-Goldring, P. (Eds.), *Evolving Explanations of Development: Ecological Approaches to Organism-Environment Systems*. American Psychological Association, Washington, DC, pp. 199–250.